THE
TWILIGHT
OF
AMERICAN
CULTURE

Social Change and Scientific Organization

Trilogy on Human Consciousness:

The Reenchantment of the World

Coming to Our Senses:
Body and Spirit in the Hidden History of the West

Wandering God:
A Study in Nomadic Spirituality

W . W . N O R T O N & C O M P A N Y | N E W Y O R K | L O N D O N

THE

TWILIGHT

OF

AMERICAN

CULTURE

MORRIS BERMAN

Excerpt from *A Canticle for Leibowitz* by William Miller reprinted by
permission of HarperCollins Publishers Inc. Copyright © 1959 by
Walter Miller, Jr. Excerpt from "This Book Is for Magda" by
Lew Welch reprinted by permission of Grey Fox Press.
Ring of Bone copyright © 1973 by Grey Fox Press.

For information about permission to reproduce selections from this book, write to
Permissions, W. W. Norton & Company, Inc.,
500 Fifth Avenue, New York, NY 10110

The text of this book is composed in Fairfield Light
with the display set in Futura Light
Composition by Molly Heron
Manufacturing by Quebecor World Book Services
Book design by JAM Design

Library of Congress Cataloging-in-Publication Data

Berman, Morris, 1944–
The twilight of American culture / Morris Berman.
p. cm.
Includes bibliographical references and index.
ISBN 0-393-04879-9
1. United States—Civilization—1970– 2. United States—Social conditions—1980–
3. Popular culture—United States. 4. Corporations—United States—Sociological
aspects. 5. Mass society. 6. Monastic and religious life—Europe—History—Middle
Ages, 600–1500. 7. Education, Humanistic—United States—Philosophy. I. Title.

E169.12.B394 2000
973.92—dc21   00-020416

W. W. Norton & Company, Inc., 500 Fifth Avenue, New York, N.Y. 10110
www.wwnorton.com

W. W. Norton & Company Ltd., 10 Coptic Street, London WC1A 1PU

3 4 5 6 7 8 9 0

FOR THREE FRIENDS:

KELLY GERLING

JANE SHOFER

JOHN WHITNEY

CONTENTS

No people can be both ignorant and free.

—Thomas Jefferson

When a population becomes distracted by trivia, when cultural life is redefined as a perpetual round of entertainments, when serious public conversation becomes a form of baby-talk, when, in short, a people become an audience and their public business a vaudeville act, then a nation finds itself at risk; culture-death is a clear possibility.

—Neil Postman,
Amusing Ourselves to Death

ACKNOWLEDGMENTS

My greatest debt is to my friend and colleague Kelly Gerling, who read the entire manuscript more than once and provided numerous suggestions and invaluable editing. Jane Shofer and Alain Carrière were also helpful in giving me detailed feedback on the original version of the book, and John Whitney was, as usual, generous with his time as my research assistant and good-natured, if relentless, as a critic. Patricia Wertman at the Library of Congress was kind enough to provide me with documents from the Congressional Research Service relevant to the entitlement question discussed in Chapter 1; Paul Dutton of Simon Fraser University steered me toward several of the sources on monasticism cited in Chapter 2; and Ann Medlock and A.T. Birmingham-Young at the Giraffe Project provided background information on a few of the "monks" described in Chapter 4. Errors that remain are my responsibility alone.

I also owe a great debt to my agent, Candice Fuhrman, who believed in this book and stood by me as we collected ironic evidence for the thesis in the form of rejection letters from publishers who, in coded form, told her that they didn't think they could make a bundle on it. Part of me was tempted to publish these in an appendix, for the reader's amusement, because, as I remarked to Candice, "they rest my case." Somehow, I refrained; but the reader should be aware if he or she is not already, that in a situation in which major conglomerates control almost all of America's intellectual property and are primarily interested in multimillion-dollar contracts for books on Bill and Monica (or whatever), this amounts to a cultural censorship almost as powerful as that which obtained in the former Soviet Union. You are, of course, free to buy and read anything you choose in the United States, but in terms of what's made available via the world of commercial publishing, 96 percent of it is pretty much the same stuff.

Which brings me to my final thank you, namely, to my editor at W. W. Norton, Robert Weil. Norton is the only major independent commercial publisher left in the United States, and Bob is probably one of the few editors still around who has this crazy idea that if there is any hope for American culture and American publishing, the bottom line is going to have to be about more than just sales. Without him, no book.

M.B.
Washington, D.C., 1999

THE
TWILIGHT
OF
AMERICAN
CULTURE

THE AMERICAN CRISIS

America has become a storefront for a corporate mob.
—Anonymous

I suppose it is a truism that authors write as much for themselves as they do for their readers. In my case—and I am assuming this is true of many other writers as well—I find the process of research and writing a way of working through certain dilemmas; of figuring out, for example, where we as a culture have been, and where we are going. For me, at least, these dilemmas are not "interesting intellectual problems" that I can explore with complete detachment, for if that were the case, I probably wouldn't bother. Rather, they are dilemmas that I feel caught up in because I am part of the cultural process I am describing. Writing thus becomes a potential mode of extrication, and I then share the results with the reader on the off chance that he or she has similar feelings. Straightforward enough, I suppose.

As the twenty-first century dawns, American culture is, quite simply, in a mess. Millions of Americans feel this, if only on a subliminal level, while a few hundred write books and articles about it, documenting the trends and analyzing the

1

causes. Titles such as Lewis Lapham's *Waiting for the Barbarians* or Robert Kaplan's *An Empire Wilderness* increasingly dot our library shelves, and excerpts from these books, and articles on these themes, find their way into some of the better national magazines. And the arguments they make are not wrong; the documentation that they provide—of crumbling school systems and widespread functional illiteracy, of violent crime and gross economic inequality, of apathy, cynicism, and what might be called "spiritual death"—is quite overwhelming. It doesn't take an Emerson or an Einstein to recognize that the system has lost its moorings, and, like ancient Rome, is drifting into an increasingly dysfunctional situation.

Still, we have ways, both individually and culturally, of hiding this from ourselves. There are so many anodynes around—such as the constant outpouring of new technological toys—and the media is brilliantly adept at drowning the country in the kinds of spectacles that keep our minds focused on the trivial and the sensational: O. J. Simpson's trial, Princess Di's death, Bill Clinton's sex life, and the CNN-style infotainment that one media rebel, David Barsamian, rightly refers to as "nuzak." But it goes deeper than this, because in an odd way, the heart of our decline is, paradoxically enough, the vitality of this culture itself. American energy is quite palpable; it's the first thing foreign visitors notice, and often admire. There is always a busyness in the air: a new film, a new scandal, a new idea to toss around (for a week), and, of course, the ever-fluctuating fortunes of the Dow. How, one might reasonably ask, can we speak of a decline, given the president's assurance, in his 1999 State of the Union speech, that the American economy is the strongest it has been in thirty years? Unemployment is down; the market is up. Our prosperity is obvious, right? What Mr. Clinton did *not* tell you, however, and what a number of analysts have documented in painstaking detail, is that the data are misleading, and deliberately so. This is a prosperity enjoyed by the rich; the reality is very different for most Americans, and almost all of the president's initiatives in the direction of economic equality were PR stunts, long on shadow, short on substance. (Once again, he "didn't inhale.") I shall say more about this in Chapter 1, but the reader should be aware that under the Clinton administration, no less than those of Reagan and Bush, the gap between rich and poor has widened dramatically, and the middle class has found itself growing smaller, and in an increasingly precarious position.

One of the things I hope to demonstrate in the pages that follow is that our much-vaunted American energy is also shadow rather than substance. It is not merely that the swirl of activity masks a core of emptiness, but that we are playing out a new version of cultural decline as described by Oswald Spengler in his famous work of 1918–22, *The Decline of the West.* Every civilization has its twilight period, said Spengler, during which it hardens into a classical phase, preserving the form of its central Idea, but losing the content, the essential spirit. Hence, Egypticism, Byzanticism, Mandarinism. In the American case, this phase has been aptly labeled (by political scientist Benjamin Barber) "McWorld"—commercial corporate consumerism for its own sake. Check out any TV ad for Nike or Pepsi and you'll see that McWorld has tremendous vitality; it appears energetic and upbeat. The problem is that since this vitality celebrates nothing substantive beyond buying and owning things, it itself *is* the cultural decline I am talking about. The United States, as Robert Kaplan suggests, is evolving into a corporate oligarchy that merely wears the trappings of a democracy. As the social critic Thomas Frank puts it, "For all the flash and cosmopolitanism of American life . . . never has it been so directly a product of the corporate imagination." In his essay "Dark Age," Frank writes:

> The wiring of every individual into the warm embrace of the
> multinational entertainment oligopoly is . . . the crowning
> triumph of the marketplace over humanity's unruly con-
> sciousness. . . . We will be able to achieve no distance from
> business culture since we will no longer have a life, a histo-
> ry, a consciousness apart from it. . . . It is putting itself
> beyond our power of imagining because it has *become* our
> imagination, it has *become* our power to envision, and
> describe, and theorize, and resist.

When we learn that corporations such as Microsoft and
AT&T are creating classroom curricula for five-year-olds, we
realize that Frank's warning cannot be dismissed as hyperbole. But until we can see this "from the outside," as it were;
until we really grasp that hype and life have merged in the
United States, we cannot do anything about it. We can only
live it out.

The concept of a vitality that is actually the touchstone of
cultural collapse is probably a strange notion to contemplate,
but when one examines the American situation more closely,
it begins to seem rather obvious. It is also an idea that is starting to surface indirectly in our culture, in some obscure
places. A film released in 1997, entitled *Love and Death on
Long Island*, which is for the most part about the obsessive
quality of romantic infatuation, develops the subtheme of the
"vital kitsch" nature of American culture quite explicitly. A
dried up British writer named Giles De'Ath (brilliantly played
by John Hurt) conceives a romantic fetish for an American
B-movie actor named Ronnie Bostock (Jason Priestley), who
stars in films with titles such as *Hotpants College 2*. In the
course of his research on Ronnie, Giles enters the world of
video rentals, tabloid journals, and home-delivery pizza—
what America does best—and finds it a refreshing change

from stodgy Victorian libraries and the predictable gray pages of the *Times Literary Supplement*. Eventually, he flies to Long Island to track down the object of his desire, who is, in fact, living with a girlfriend. Undeterred, Giles subtly courts him, finally proposing that Ronnie return with him to England and pick up his acting career in Europe. When Ronnie balks, saying that all of his contacts are in the United States, and that "this is where I am known," Giles counters, "As *what*, Ronnie? As *what*?" Love-struck or not, Giles is no one's fool; he understands that what attracts him about "Bostock Nation," its youthful energy, is at the same time devoid of any real purpose beyond the generation of that energy. Ronnie, for his part, knows he's no John Gielgud, and so they go their separate ways.

Another locus of this theme, of the decline that shows up as pseudorenewal, is the work of Don DeLillo, particularly his novel *White Noise*. The book is quite literally a masterpiece, portraying as it does a busy commercial culture that is riddled with purposelessness and paranoia. The central character, Jack Gladney, a college professor of "Hitler Studies," discovers his young daughter talking in her sleep, whispering the words "Toyota Celica." A lethal black cloud, or "toxic event," as it is called, gets mysteriously released into the atmosphere, acting as a metaphor for the white noise that has become a total environment—radio and TV emissions, microwaves, cyberwaves, police sirens, electronic noises from video games and appliances—all of which are pulsing with life, but which are actually harbingers of death. Throughout the novel is the repetition of American commercial "triads": Dacron, Orlon, Lycra Spandex; MasterCard, Visa, American Express; Leaded, Unleaded, Super Unleaded, underscoring the commercial frenzy of it all with a recurring, rhythmic beat. In a shopping mall, Jack stops suddenly and thinks to himself:

I realized the place was awash in noise. The toneless systems, the jangle and skid of carts, the loudspeaker and coffee-making machines, the cries of children. And over it all, or under it all, a dull and unlocatable roar, as of some form of swarming life just outside the range of human apprehension.

"The networks, the circuits, the streams, the harmonies," he thinks to himself appreciatively, after checking his bank balance at an ATM. "The system was invisible, which made it all the more impressive. . . ."

This notion of invisibility—of no one in this glorious new age of corporate cyberglobalism being to blame because the system is not really located anywhere (but everywhere)—is important for an understanding of the present crisis of American culture I shall be describing in this book. This crisis is the logical culmination of a certain historical process that began in Europe at the end of the Middle Ages, expanded during the Scientific and Industrial Revolutions, and finally climaxed in our own time. These developments were immensely creative, but they did carry a kind of "vector" that led to the triumph of global corporate hegemony, the information superhighway, and the culture of McWorld, in which everything is drowned in the universal solvent of kitsch and consumerism, white noise and Bostockiana. As already indicated, I am going to point to a possible way out of this morass, but the reader needs to be aware of the structural nature of this malaise. It developed "geologically," as it were, in slow, cumulative accretions, and trendy formulas for change, ranging from "paradigm shifts" to recycling your newspapers, are simply not going to cut it. Americans, of course, love pap, and they will pay huge sums to hear that things are not *really* so bad, and that they can be quickly and "spiritually" repaired. But structural problems require structural solutions, and it is for this reason that we must—despite the noble intentions of their authors—reject books such as Marianne Williamson's *The Healing of America*, which promise the reader a short-term panacea based on "spiritual awakening," or those like Gerry Spence's *Give Me Liberty!*, which argue for major changes based on legislation, grassroots activism, and an act of will. I certainly have no quarrel with grassroots activism (Spence's Trial Lawyer's College, designed to train "people's lawyers," is a fine project, for example), but let's not kid ourselves: The ability of these sorts of approaches to significantly deflect the juggernaut of global corporate capitalism in a decade or two is nonexistent, and there can be no healing in false optimism or in avoidance of the truth. It is the truth itself that is healing, not New Age dreams or populist fantasies. And the truth is that *real change is historical*, and if one is going to point to, say, the collapse of the Soviet Union as an example of a "sudden" liberatory event, let us remember that that collapse was seventy-three years in the making, and finally happened because of structural inconsistencies that couldn't be fended off any longer. Recovery exists only in the long term, and the "healing of America" will come about concomitantly with structural changes in the economy. The same is true of all the advanced industrial nations. Thus when Oskar Lafontaine, Germany's minister of finance, attempted early in 1999 to impose higher taxes on industry and to resist attempts to scale down social welfare programs, businesses threatened to leave and the German economy suffered a brief downturn. Herr Lafontaine finally resigned, and the *Washington Post* editorialized (15 March 1999) that the resignation "shows the limits of any single politician, or any single country, to stem the tide of global capitalism."

"The enduring achievement of historical study," wrote the eminent British historian, Sir Lewis Namier, "is a historical sense—an intuitive understanding—of how things do *not* happen" (italics mine). The dissolution of corporate hegemony, when it does occur—and our own "Soviet watershed" is at least forty or fifty years down the road, as of this writing—will happen because of the ultimate inability of the system to maintain itself indefinitely. This type of breakdown, which is a recurrent historical phenomenon, is a long-range one and internal to the system; it does not come about because 300,000 people meditated or "shifted their paradigm" or supported their independent food co-op. I call this "realistic optimism."

Of course, books that argue for rapid substantive change reflect not only popular American naïveté but also an understandable impatience with the fact that history rarely moves as fast as a single human life. My own solution to our contemporary cultural crisis—what I call the "monastic option"—is certainly a long shot, but at least there is some historical precedent for deliberate acts of cultural preservation forming a geological accretion of their own and eventually turning things around. If nothing else, such activity will make a perceptible difference for the individuals who undertake it; and it may, just possibly, have a larger unanticipated effect. The word *twilight*, after all, implies an eventual dawn, and at some point we are going to emerge from our contemporary twilight and future darkness, if only because *no* historical configuration is the end of history.

What is the historical precedent I am talking about? Although it is a rather convoluted story (see Chapter 2), I am referring to a group of individuals—specifically, monks—who were not able to fit into the disintegrating landscape of the Roman Empire, and who experienced themselves as strangers in a strange land. What Roman culture had discarded, these monks treated as valuable; what the culture found worthwhile, they perceived as stupid or destructive. And so, beginning in the fourth century A.D., these men took it upon themselves to preserve the treasures of Greco-Roman civilization as the lights of their own culture were rapidly fading. In Ireland, and on the Continent, they sequestered and copied the books and manuscripts that represented the greatest cultural achievements of that civilization—material that, six hundred years later, proved to be a crucial factor in the dawn of a new European culture.

If such people were badly needed in the fourth century and after to keep European civilization from disappearing altogether, we surely need them today, as the English novelist E. M. Forster recognized as early as 1939 in his seminal essay, *What I Believe.* "I believe in aristocracy," he wrote,

> . . . Not an aristocracy of power, based upon rank and influence, but an aristocracy of the sensitive, the considerate and the plucky. Its members are to be found in all nations and classes, and all through the ages, and there is a secret understanding between them when they meet. They represent the true human tradition, the one permanent victory of our queer race over cruelty and chaos. . . . On they go—an invincible army, yet not a victorious one. The aristocrats, the elect, the chosen, the Best People—all the words that describe them are false, and all attempts to organize them fail. Again and again Authority, seeing their value, has tried to net them and to utilize them as the Egyptian Priesthood or the Christian Church or the Chinese Civil Service or the Group Movement, or some other worthy stunt. But they slip through the net and are gone; when the door is shut, they are no longer in the room; their temple . . . is the Holiness of the Heart's Imagination, and their kingdom, though they never possess it, is the wide-open world.

When I speak of a new, contemporary class of monks (see Chapter 4), I do not, of course, mean that literally. I am not

talking about asceticism or religious practice, and certainly not
organization into monastic orders. But I *am* talking about
renunciation. Today's "monk" is determined to resist the spin
and hype of the global corporate world order; he or she knows
the difference between reality and theme parks, integrity and
commercial promotion. He regards Starbucks as a sad plastic
replica of the gritty (or bohemian) café of bygone days. She has
no truck with the trendy "wisdom" of the New Age, and instead
seeks guidance about the human condition from Flaubert or
Virginia Woolf, rather than from the latest guru tossed up by
the media or the counterculture. Computers and the Internet
are, for such a person, useful tools, not a way of life, and she
understands that both the Republican and Democratic parties
represent corporate interests, rather than genuine democracy.
She has no problem being labeled an elitist, because she
agrees with Garrison Keillor that "what's really snooty is to put
out commercial garbage for an audience that you yourself feel
superior to." The new monk is a sacred/secular humanist, dedicated not to slogans or the fashionable patois of postmodernism, but to Enlightenment values that lie at the heart of our
civilization: the disinterested pursuit of the truth, the cultiva-
tion of art, the commitment to critical thinking, inter alia.
Above all, he knows the difference between quality and kitsch,
and he seeks to preserve the former in the teeth of a culture
that is drowning in the latter. If she is a high school teacher,
she has her class reading the *Odyssey*, despite the fact that
half the teachers in the school have assigned Danielle Steel. If
he is a writer, he writes for posterity, not for the best-seller lists.
As a mother, she takes her kids camping or to art museums,
not to *Pocahontas*. He elects, in short, to save his life via the
monastic option.

One word by way of disclaimer, however, before I get to the
heart of the argument: I am not maintaining that all organized,

institutional opposition to the dominant culture is a waste of time. I doubt it will produce any significant results in the short run, but by and large, no one can know for certain what the long-term effect of any effort is going to be. To take a personal example, for some months I worked as a reading and writing tutor in a Washington, D.C., charter high school for black teenagers at risk with the law, a school that had been started to give such kids a better option than jail. It was, for the most part, a thankless task: These students came from violent and drug-ridden backgrounds, knew that the deck was stacked against them, and were sullen and apathetic as a result. I had a few small victories, but most of my charges were not going to let themselves be drawn. (It was not a race issue, either; they were intractable to the black instructors as well.) Poverty and violence had drained them of any curiosity about the world; some of them, at age sixteen or seventeen, had never heard of the Atlantic Ocean, did not know what 1999 meant, historically speaking, or thought the Civil War had taken place in the 1960s. One student thought that Washington, D.C., was in the Midwest, and was not able to locate New York, Florida, or Texas on a sketchy map I drew of the United States. Nor could these students see why they should bother themselves about such things in any case. But how can one be seventeen years old, live less than one hundred miles from the Atlantic Ocean, and not have ever even heard of it, or be living in D.C. and think it is in Nebraska? This is not cultural deprivation; it is cultural massacre. It seemed to me that the best the school could do was to fish a few of the least deprived kids out of the drink, but that the larger social reality was going to remain unaffected.

Should we not have such schools? Should I have turned down the offer to work there? One thing I admired was the attitude of the cofounder, an attorney in his early thirties who was full of beans and who had posted a Chinese proverb (from Confucius, I believe) outside his office: "Those who say it cannot be done need to get out of the way of the people who are doing it." Questioned privately, Tom (not his real name) admitted to me that he doubted that the school could really make a difference in the larger scheme of things. Economic oppression, a corporate system that ruthlessly divides people into a handful of winners and an army of losers on an uneven playing field, really works; its ability to grind people into the dirt, to crush their spirit almost completely, is quite impressive, when you see it up close. It is no accident that the odds of an African-American male age eighteen to twenty-four winding up in jail is significantly greater than his winding up in college. But both Tom and I agreed that the odds notwithstanding, it made more sense to set up a school to try to beat those statistics than to do nothing at all. What I admired about Tom was that he was not living in la-la land, hyping the "healing of America" in ten easy steps. He *knew* it was a long shot. The point is, what *else* should he do with his life?

So I am not rejecting group or institutional solutions out of hand. Who, for example, would dispute the value of Amnesty International, or—in my view at least—a revitalized labor movement? My skepticism concerns the larger impact of such groups, and I remain much more sanguine about the long-term impact of individual commitment, what I am calling the monastic option, but in a modern incarnation. And while I do not regard *elitism* as a dirty word, I have to add that the monastic option is not about class and privilege—not at all. Earl Shorris ran a Great Books program for the inner-city poor in New York, and it was a resounding success. My motto is something akin to a line from the French philosopher Jean-François Lyotard: elitism for everybody. Or as the founder of the original

Great Books program at the University of Chicago, Robert Maynard Hutchins, once put it, "The best education for the best is the best education for all."

This is, then, a book for oddballs, for men and women who experience themselves as expatriates within their own country. It is a guidebook of sorts, to the twenty-first century and beyond. It seeks to give the reader a sense of where we are, in historical terms, and what this means; a way of orienting him- or herself to contemporary events, so as to be able to find meaning in a disintegrating culture, and perhaps to contribute in some way to the eventual reconstruction of that culture on a very different basis. What I hope to show is that in long-range terms at least, there is reason to hope. As damaged as Americans are, as dulled as their senses are from the endless bombardment of white noise and infotainment, I am convinced that there remains a vital core within us all that hungers for reality, that knows the difference between the cotton-candy world of Bostock Nation and the dense, opaque world of difficult thinking, challenging living. If this distinction makes intuitive sense to you; if you have finally had it with CNN and Hollywood and John Grisham and New Age "spirituality," then pull up a chair, unplug your phone (beeper, TV, fax machine, computer, etc.), and give me a few hours of your time. I promise to do my best not to entertain you.

O N E

COLLAPSE, OR
TRANSFORMATION?

Sallust's description of Rome in 80 B.C.—a government controlled by wealth, a ruling-class numb to the repetitions of political scandal, a public diverted by chariot races and gladiatorial shows—stands as a fair summary of some of our own circumstances. . . .

—Lewis Lapham,
Waiting for the Barbarians

Before we can talk about the long road to cultural healing, then, we must begin by understanding the illness. But here we are confronted with a complicating factor, briefly alluded to in the Introduction: Decline comes inevitably to all civilizations. With the exception of hunter-gatherer societies that have not been interfered with by more complex ones (and there are no pristine hunter-gatherers left anymore, I fear), the pattern of birth, maturity, and decay would seem to be inescapable. *Est ubi gloria nunc Babyloniae?* Where is the glory of Babylonia now? Or that of ancient Egypt, China, India, Greece, Rome? Gone, all gone—that is the historical record. Why, then, should America escape this fate? If decay is built into the civilizational process itself, then talk of healing might be a bit out of place. Indeed, from an analytical standpoint, the problem is not that states collapse—for that is the rule—but that some manage to last as long as they do. To what purpose, then, my attempt to give the reader a cultural roadmap, or to suggest a way out, a creative response? If the historical record is clear on this point, there *is* no way out. We might just as well fiddle while New York and Los Angeles burn.

This is, of course, a formidable objection, one not easily dismissed. Nor do I believe that America is somehow so privileged as to constitute a historical exception (which belief would be a typically American kind of hubris). But three things do jump out of the historical record that are worth mentioning. First, the process of decay may be inevitable, but it is rarely linear. In its three thousand years, for example, Egypt suffered periods of complete political disintegration and foreign domination that sometimes lasted more than a century, and it then bounced back. While its ultimate decline was inevitable, and it was eventually absorbed into the Greco-Roman Empire, three millennia is not exactly an unimpressive showing; and most of those years were "up" (in terms of political coherence), while some of them were "down." So it might conceivably be argued that the United States is going through a bad patch, from which it might recover, at least for a time.

Second, if the classical model of collapse of empire is that of ancient Rome, we have to remember that its fall was, in terms of the larger world system, as much a transformation as it was a decline. Indeed, it was from the ruins of the Roman Empire that medieval European civilization emerged. While the parallels between the Roman case and the American one are not exact, the analogy does suggest some transformative possibilities. If, for example, we are indeed slated for another dark age, it may not have to last six hundred years this time around. This is precisely a case in which something like the monastic option, and the deliberate work of cultural preservation, might come into play.

Third, there is the issue already mentioned in the Introduction, and which I shall discuss later on in this chapter, as well: This is a very lively kind of decline. In this sense, possible hubris notwithstanding, something unprecedented *might* be happening. Europe's Dark Ages were truly dark—"singularly monochromatic," as the historian Peter Brown put it. Our own transformation is confusing, because of the "invisibility" factor discussed above. For those seduced by noise, toys, and technology, the current transformation to a global economy is nothing less than cultural efflorescence. For those who place their values elsewhere, there is the paradox that the very success of McWorld, the very transformation that it represents, is a darkness that is ultimately every bit as dark as the early Middle Ages, no matter what the surface appearances might indicate. Whether this will make recovery easier or more difficult remains to be seen.

My point, in other words, is that even if decline is historically inevitable, it is still a process that contains unexpected twists and turns. The sine curve may be descending, but there are loopholes in it nonetheless. Furthermore, the precedent of the monastic option suggests that there might be ways of ensuring that what is of value in this civilization can be preserved and handed down in the hope of generating cultural renewal at some later point. As for the individual reader poring over these pages, he or she doesn't *have* to be a statistic; there are choices to be made that move in directions opposite to the general tide of events. Before we discuss all that, however, we need to have a closer look at the larger process of civilizational decline, and the factors that come into play when a culture enters its twilight phase and begins to implode.

The concept of decline often involves organic metaphors, notions of birth, maturity, and senescence. This way of viewing civilization goes back to the eighteenth century (Giambattista

Vico), and perhaps even to the ancient Greeks; but it came into common currency in the nineteenth century through the writings of the German Idealist school of philosophy. Hegel, for example, saw history as a kind of spiritual journey, in which *Geist* ("spirit") moved around the globe, generating the Renaissance in fifteenth-century Florence, and sowing the seeds of decay when it subsequently departed. Oswald Spengler, as already noted, thought in similar terms, arguing that a civilization was organized around a central ideal, or some sort of Platonic Idea, and that the process of civilization involved a stage of aging, during which the Idea hardened into pure form. Writing in the early twentieth century, Spengler believed that this process of formalism, or "classicism," as he called it, was happening to the West during his lifetime, and that it would be on the Western agenda for the next few centuries.

There is, perhaps, something intellectually satisfying about the organic approach. After all, humans die, so why not civilizations? It is, however, not really necessary to rely on organic metaphors (or mystical forces) as sources of explanation. As Joseph Tainter points out in *The Collapse of Complex Societies*, civilizations are anomalies. The whole statist configuration of hierarchy, specialization, and bureaucracy emerged fairly recently—about six thousand years ago—and has to be constantly reinforced and legitimized. It also requires an expanding material base and a constant mobilization of resources, and the trend is always toward higher levels of complexity. There is the processing of greater quantities of information and energy, the formation of larger settlements, increasing class differentiation and stratification, and the development of more complex technology. Collapse, which involves a progressive weakening of the political and administrative center, is the reversal of all this, and a recurrent feature of human societies. As the center weakens, there is no longer an "umbrella" to guarantee safety. The strong savage the weak, and there is no higher goal than survival. Literacy may be lost entirely, or decline so dramatically that a dark age is inevitable.

Thus collapse is built into the process of civilization itself, but this can be understood in purely rational or economic terms. When stress—for example, resource shortage—emerges in hunter-gatherer societies, the members of the tribe have an easy option, one that worked for hundreds of millennia: They move. The solution, in short, is horizontal (dispersion). But if you are sedentary, committed to staying in one place and depending on that place for your livelihood, you must "go vertical," that is, generate another level of hierarchical control to solve your problems—a process that never ends. The whole thing is cumulative. Taxes rarely go down; information processing gets denser. Standing armies get larger, not smaller, and bureaucracies grow rather than shrink. Elites want—and get—more and more of the pie, and so forth. What is unleashed is an unending spiral of increasing complexity and correspondingly higher costs. Finally, says Tainter, "investment in sociopolitical complexity as a problem-solving response often reaches a point of declining marginal returns." The "center of gravity" is too high; the benefits per unit of investment start to drop off. At this point—that of diminishing returns—collapse is not only inevitable; it actually becomes economical. Although the effects are not exactly pleasant, collapse finally becomes an economizing process, the best adaptation under the circumstances.

Tainter's argument, however, is not necessarily at odds with that the of German Idealists. For one thing, both he and Spengler agree that collapse is inherent to the process of civilization itself, and thus inevitable. But there is even deeper agreement than this, although it is implicit: Economic decline has an obvious "spiritual" component, which shows up as apathy and meaninglessness—what the French sociologist Emile Durkheim called "anomie," and which is the reality lurking beneath the facade of Spengler's classicism. In the classicist phase, the culture no longer believes in itself, so it typically undertakes phony or misguided wars (Vietnam, or the Gulf War of 1991, for example), or promotes its symbols and slogans all the more. As the organizational costs rise, yielding increasingly smaller benefits, so does the formalism, the pomp and circumstance. Just as the jaded crowds of ancient Rome zoned out on bread and circuses, Hollywood makes *Rocky*-type films, rerunning tired old formulas, but nevertheless, these are box-office hits. And gladiatorial extravaganzas, as well as the "Rambification" of culture, are sure signs of spiritual death.

If we can pull together the threads of this discussion so far, it would seem that four factors are present when a civilization collapses:

(a) Accelerating social and economic inequality
(b) Declining marginal returns with regard to investment in organizational solutions to socioeconomic problems
(c) Rapidly dropping levels of literacy, critical understanding, and general intellectual awareness
(d) Spiritual death—that is, Spengler's classicism: the emptying out of cultural content and the freezing (or repackaging) of it in formulas—kitsch, in short.

It is at this point that this scenario may strike the reader as hauntingly familiar, because these four conditions would seem to apply to the United States at the beginning of the twenty-first century. What reader of these pages is not aware that the gap between rich and poor has increasingly widened since the 1970s? That entitlements such as Social Security are under threat, or that we incarcerate more people per capita (565 per

100,000) than any other country in the world? That millions of our high school graduates can barely read or write, and that common words are now often misspelled on public signs? That community life has been reduced to shopping malls, and that most Americans grow old in isolation, zoning out in front of TV screens, and/or on antidepressant drugs? This is the nitty-gritty, daily reality that belies the glitz and glamour of the so-called New World Order.

In order to understand the reality of our situation, it will be necessary to flesh these four factors out in some detail. But—to skip ahead for a moment—it is, once again, not a simple case of civilizational collapse, but a more complex one of cultural transformation. Viewed from a certain perspective—that of Wall Street, Beverly Hills, the region contained within the Capital Beltway, and Redmond, Washington (home of Microsoft)—the transformation to the global society of the twenty-first century is a great success. In terms of late-empire developments, with the Soviet Union now a vestige of the past, it may even be adaptive, at least for another fifty or one hundred years. After all, if there is nobody around to offer a different definition of success, then perhaps there really isn't a problem. The meaning of *collapse* is in the eye of the beholder, *n'est-ce pas?*

Let us take a closer look at what the American transformation consists of. I shall begin with the data on social inequality, Item (a).

There was a time, not so long ago, when data on rich versus poor could only be found in left-wing journals. I remember how, as graduate students in the sixties, we would excitedly photocopy these articles and distribute them to our friends. Today, this is all just basic information, often obtainable from mainstream newspapers or the pages of journals such as

Business Week and *Fortune*. In a 1995 article in *The New Yorker*, John Cassidy notes that between 1947 and 1973, while there was certainly a great disparity between rich and poor, actual incomes rose at the same rate for everyone. In that sense, the increase of income mapped across the five quintiles of society, and arranged on a graph, looked like a picket fence. But from 1973 to 1993, he says, it was only the highest quintile, the rich, that enjoyed a significant increase in wealth. The top 1 percent of the nation saw its income level grow 78 percent between 1977 and 1989, and Federal Reserve Board figures from 1989 reveal that this elite group owned 40 percent of the nation's wealth. By 1995, according to Robert Reich, the figure (excluding the value of homes) had risen to 47 percent—more than $4 trillion in assets—while the upper quintile owned 93 percent. The result is that America is no longer a middle-class society. "The picket fence," Cassidy remarks, "has been replaced by a small staircase, and some of the staircase is underground." The two lowest quintiles (bottom 40 percent) experienced a decline in income during the period from 1973 to 1993, whereas the top quintile saw a transfer of $275 billion per year from the middle class to the rich. In 1973, the typical CEO of a large company earned about forty times what a typical worker did; today, he earns from 190 to 419 times as much. Reich notes that Bill Gates' net worth in 1998—$46 billion—was larger than the combined net worth of the bottom 40 percent of American households. What the country has experienced, concludes Cassidy, is "an unprecedented redistribution of income toward the rich." In terms of wealth disparity, the United States leads all other major industrial nations.

MIT economist Paul Krugman refers to this trend as a "spiral of inequality," with economic lopsidedness increasing every year. As it gets increasingly difficult for most Americans to make a living, it also becomes increasingly easier for a select handful to make a killing. According to the Census Bureau, the bottom 20 percent of U.S. families in 1970 received 5.4 percent of the national income, while the top 5 percent received 15.6 percent. By 1994, the corresponding figures were 4.2 percent and 20.1 percent. All of this, says Krugman, signals a "seismic shift in the character of our society." It also indicates a shift in our values. In 1962, President Kennedy confronted the U.S. Steel Corporation over price increases and forced it to back down. Today, upper-echelon CEOs would be more likely to be invited to dinner at the White House.

As far as the White House goes, messages from it about the increasing prosperity of Americans have to be taken with several pounds of salt. "While the national economy has been growing," writes William Finnegan (*Cold New World*), "the economic prospects of most Americans have been dimming."

Yes, by 1999 the unemployment rate was the lowest it had been in twenty-five years, but during that same time period real hourly wages fell significantly, the median household income went down, and the national poverty rate rose. The number of low-wage jobs proliferated dramatically. The past twenty-five years, notes Finnegan, have produced "the first generation-long decline in the average worker's wages in American history. . . . The middle class, defined by almost any measure, has been shrinking conspicuously for some time." Thus the White House boast that 70 percent of the workers who lost their jobs between 1993 and 1995 found new ones by early 1996 is hollow, for the great majority of that 70 percent found only part-time jobs or ones paying less than their previous wages. Since 1979, 43 million jobs have been erased in the United States.

We are, in short, drifting toward a situation such as exists in India, or Mexico, or Brazil, and nothing is being done to halt this. During the period from 1991 to 1994, for example, the number of Mexican billionaires went from two to twenty-eight.

Ernesto Canales Santos, a corporate attorney who has represented many of these men, calls it "the Aztec pyramid model," much of which was made possible by U.S. investment, and which, in turn, had repercussions for our own lopsideness. Thus David Calleo (*The Bankrupting of America*) writes: "The advanced part of the [American] economy seems a more and more prosperous enclave, barricaded within a deteriorating nation. Rather than providing a model for the third world, the United States appears to be imitating it." "If anything," adds David Rieff of the World Policy Institute, "America, with its widening income gap, its vast, deepening divergences in everything from education to life expectancy between rich and poor, is less democratic today . . . than it was in 1950."

The effect of these trends, and of growing corporate hegemony, has been particularly devastating on children—not only in the United States, but in other parts of the world as well. Between 1979 and 1990, the number of American children living below the poverty line rose an astonishing 22 percent. A 1996 article entitled "India's Child Slaves," in the *International Herald Tribune*, notes that 15 million children in India work eleven to twelve hours daily in dangerous conditions, and are beaten if they try to escape. In the silk industry—financed by the World Bank—children as young as six and seven years of age are forced to plunge their hands into scalding water. To avoid starvation, many Indian families send their handicapped offspring to wealthy Arab nations to beg. Girls under ten are sold into prostitution, and India is hardly alone in this (Asian countries employ an estimated 1 million child prostitutes). Worldwide, according to the UN's International Labor Organization, 250 million children between the ages of five and fourteen are now employed across Asia, Africa, and Latin America, and this involves slavery, prostitution, and work in hazardous industries.

Events such as these do not happen in a vacuum. Involvement of the World Bank, and/or U.S. corporations, is part of the whole fabric of oppression. Global corporate hegemony, multinational and transnational in nature, means by definition that these events are linked by a web of interdependent markets, investments, and trade agreements. The wealth of America's top quintile is implicated not only in the poverty of South Central Los Angeles but also in the slums of Buenos Aires. In 1991, the Nike Corporation made $3 billion in profits, paying its factory workers in Indonesia—mostly poor, malnourished women—$1.03 a day, not enough for food and shelter. (Just *do* it!) By 1996, the 447 richest people on the planet had assets equal to that of the poorest 2.5 billion—42 percent of the world population. What do we think it means when we buy a new sweater and the label reads MADE IN THE PHILIPPINES, or a transistor radio stamped MADE IN KOREA? What do we imagine the social and economic reality is behind these seemingly neutral words? Or behind the cup of Colombian (Brazilian, Angolan, etc.) supremo that we drink every morning, or the cleverly crafted decaf latte with 2 percent milk that we enjoy on a sunny autumn afternoon in a chic café with our friends? We hardly need Ann Landers to tell us to "wake up and smell the coffee." The truth is that it is a bitter brew; that the affluence of the few is purchased at the misery of the many.

The argument that world inequality is structural is a major theme of what is known as world-systems analysis, which views the drama in terms of a distinction between core and periphery. Core countries are those in the privileged regions of the Northern Hemisphere such as the United States and Western Europe. It is in these regions that financial, technical, and productive (usually industrial) power is concentrated, power that is controlled by an elite. The periphery, on the other hand, contains the exploited regions that sell their resources and labor to the core without ever having access to the latter's wealth. The enrichment of the core is structurally dependent on the impoverishment of the periphery. Thus today, the Pacific periphery consists of Burma, Thailand, Malaysia, Indonesia, and the Philippines, whereas Europe's periphery is largely Africa, what the French economist Jacques Attali (in *Millennium*), calls "an economic black hole." In a future world of, say, 8 billion people by A.D. 2050 (a very conservative estimate, incidentally), Attali believes that 5 billion of these will, because of this structural inequality, be living right at the survival line, just managing to hang on. The twenty-first century, he writes, will be a *Blade Runner* world, "a world that has embraced a common ideology of consumerism but is bitterly divided between rich and poor." The latter, inhabiting the destitute peripheries, will be "boat people living on a planetary scale." But, he adds, this situation is highly volatile, because those in the periphery are increasingly aware that the prosperity of the core is purchased at their expense. They will, as a result, eventually rise up against the core in "a war unlike any seen in modern times."

Sociologist Christopher Chase-Dunn has pursued this theme in great detail in his book *Global Formation*. He shows that the core/periphery hierarchy is a structural feature of the world system, that is, it is an institution of socially structured inequality. Historically, going back to the Commercial Revolution of the sixteenth century and the plunder of the Americas, the exploitation of the periphery was crucially important to the emergence of industrial capitalism in the core, and the direct use of coercive force eventually evolved into institutionalized economic power based on "law" and private property. So a network of interdependent markets is the main glue of our global system, he says, bolstered, when necessary, by the military power of the core states. Thus, we read in American newspapers (*Seattle Post-Intelligencer*, 27 January 1997; originally reported in the *Baltimore Sun* in 1995) of a CIA training manual that decribes torture methods used in Honduras during the 1980s. This was part of President Reagan's effort to control leftist movements in Nicaragua and El Salvador; movements that were, like the subsequent uprisings in Mexico (Chiapas), fighting for local self-determination and against those market forces trying to grind them down into permanent peripheral status. Or consider the situation in Colombia, where according to the Human Rights Watch, CIA officials helped the government set up "killer networks" of paramilitary soldiers for the purpose of murdering suspected leftists, as well as supplying arms and money for this purpose.

No surprise here, of course; this is an old story in our relationship with Latin America. Nevertheless, writes Chase-Dunn, political coercion coming directly from the core has become less central to the structure of exploitation and domination, since the core can rely on *local* coercion—that is, authoritarian client states in the periphery to do its dirty work in exchange for economic aid to the elite in the periphery; and economic exploitation, organized through the production and sale of commodities, is a more efficient, "less dirty," means of control. (Add to this, in recent years, the role of the World Bank, the International Monetary Fund, NAFTA, GATT, the proposed Multilateral Agreement on Investment, and so on.)

In any case, the system is a nested one, with wheels within wheels. There are important inequalities between major areas of the globe, but also within specific regions. Thus the peripheral countries of Brazil and Nigeria play the role of core countries vis-à-vis nations peripheral to *them*. All of this, in turn, ricochets back onto the core sectors within the core countries. Exploitation of the periphery, and the threat of the flight of capital to the latter, has served to keep labor unions and socialist parties docile, preventing them from successfully challenging elite powers within the core.

All of this is part and parcel of the global economy. Thus, Federal Reserve Board Chairman Alan Greenspan, in congressional testimony given on 21 January 1997, said that "heightened job insecurity explains a significant part of the restraint on compensation [that is, wages] and the consequent muted price inflation." Typically, when employment increases, the Dow-Jones average falls. For the economic elite in the core, it pays to have an insecure labor force.

Both the penetration of a peripheral nation by foreign investment and the creation of debt dependence by means of foreign credit actually serve to damage that nation's economic development, and to increase inequality within that country. The net effect is the replacement of direct colonial control by neocolonial economic mechanisms. The structure of dependency, says Chase-Dunn, "provides support for elites in the periphery and keeps wages low relative to the income of elites." These elites, in fact, are linked "to the interest of the transnational corporations and the international economy," not to their own nations or people.

For the purposes of our own discussion, however, it is important to remember that this description also applies to peripheral areas within the United States, not just, say, to Guatemala. Month by month, more and more wealth is being transferred to fewer and fewer hands. In mid-1997, Republicans in Congress proposed a tax cut that was designed to give the upper quintile 87 percent of the tax savings over the next decade. Two years later the attempt was repeated when the House and Senate passed a compromise tax bill, which would give the richest quintile 79 percent of the tax savings, as well as pass billions of dollars in tax breaks on to multinational corporations. The process is inexorable; and although I would not

predict a massive popular uprising within the United States—
that is more likely to happen in peripheral regions outside the
core countries—it is nevertheless true that this kind of
inequality could eventually destroy the entire social fabric, as
it nearly has already in the case of public schools and inner
cities. It is also spiritually corrosive, demoralizing, and will do
untold damage to this nation. In this regard, if one wants to
make a comparison with ancient Rome, it is interesting to note
that during the reign of Nero (A.D. 54–68) roughly two thousand men owned nearly all of the land between the Rhine and
the Euphrates. The population was pretty much divided
between the rich and all the rest, and the rich were very, very
rich. Similarly, writes Kevin Phillips (in *Arrogant Capital*), what
we are witnessing in the United States today is a broad transition "toward social and economic stratification, toward walled-
in communities and hardening class structures, [and] toward
political, business and financial elites that bail each other
out. . . ."

Why is this slide toward greater inequality occurring? Partly, it is because the concentration of wealth in fewer and fewer
hands is itself part of the process of declining marginal returns.
Every time a greater investment in complexity takes place, it
is accompanied by a greater share of the pie for the elite. Hierarchy generates power; the greater the verticality, the greater
the opportunity for the few to exploit the many, especially in
times of debt and crisis. "As massive debt becomes a major
national problem," writes Kevin Phillips, "it also becomes a
major financial opportunity and vested interest." For a select
few, in other words, national collapse is a good business opportunity! But ultimately, no one knows exactly why America has
experienced such a shift in wealth, as John Cassidy admits. It
seems to be due to a combination of factors: the rising volume
of international trade, the spread of computer technology, the

decline of labor unions, and the immigration of unskilled workers into the country. Yet all of these factors are controversial,
and a truly unambiguous explanation escapes us. The best that
any economist can say is that this is just how capitalism has
developed (or in the case of Rome, perhaps it was just a function of the closing phase of empire). The only thing that can
reverse this trend, besides a dramatic revitalization of labor
unions, would be a very steep tax on the rich. In the mid-
1990s, Robert Reich, who was then Secretary of Labor, floated
this out as a possibility, and his suggestion was met with a deaf-
ening silence. There simply is no sympathy for such a solution,
even among middle-class citizens for whom such a move
would be an obvious benefit (largely because, I suspect, they
individually believe that they alone will somehow beat the system and become rich themselves—sort of like winning the
lottery). As a result, the progressive "Aztecization" of the country is a foregone conclusion.

Let us, then, turn to Item (b), the Tainter thesis as it applies
to the American economy. If we focus on what is probably the
major issue here, that of entitlements—principally Social
Security and Medicare—we discover that this is, unfortunately, a very murky area. As far as entitlements go, the data and
prognoses seem to change almost every month. Hence, by the
time this book appears in print, my data will probably be obsolete. In addition, in this particular area, the data can vary significantly depending on the political agenda of the researcher.
Position papers published by right-wing think tanks—the Cato
Institute, the Heritage Foundation, the National Center for
Policy Analysis—argue that the entitlement system is in a crisis situation and that a program such as Social Security needs
to be phased out and/or totally overhauled. Hence, we have to
be wary of the data here, because they are often a front for

privatization—for example, replacing Social Security with private pensions along the lines of IRAs or 401(k) plans. At the other end of the spectrum, such as it exists in the United States, we have the Brookings Institution, which argues that the system needs only moderate adjustments to stay on track. So it is hard to decide which arguments are valid, given these competing claims, and the reader should be aware that I am not an economist, or any sort of expert in these matters. Let me take a shot at it, nonetheless.

In some ways, the best place to start is with the reports of the Social Security Administration (SSA) itself. According to the trustees' report of 30 March 1999, Social Security will become insolvent in 2034, and the Hospital Insurance part of Medicare will do so by 2015. The combined expenditures here are higher than the taxes and premiums collected to support them, and this situation will continue. Thus the cost of these, which is 7 percent of the Gross Domestic Product (GDP) today, will rise to 11.7 percent by 2030. By 2025, claims on the Social Security trust fund will be $86 billion, and by 2075, costs for Medicare will be 45 percent higher than the income available for it. These figures, moreover, are not based on a particularly pessimistic scenario. In fact, as early as 2014, other federal receipts will be needed to help pay benefits. Hence, comments a Congressional Research Service (CRS) report on the situation, "the long-range outlook . . . leaves little to be sanguine about," and popular opinion reflects this. Less than 50 percent of the American people believe that Social Security will meet its long-term commitments, and in the group of those below age fifty-five, nearly two-thirds have little confidence that it will work for them.

Why is this the case? The answer is obvious: We are becoming an older nation. By 2025, the number of people sixty-five years and older will grow by 75 percent, whereas the number

of workers supporting the system will grow by only 13 percent. The current ratio of workers to Social Security recipi-
ents is 3.4:1; by 2035, it will drop to 2:1. The "big three"
entitlements—Social Security, Medicare, and Medicaid—will
grow rapidly burdensome because the costs are directly linked
to an aging population.

Turning to the reports of conservative organizations, such
as those previously mentioned, the most pessimistic scenario
of the SSA, they point out, is that by 2045 almost 53 percent
of the total taxable payroll in the United States will be needed
to fund Social Security and Medicare. Whereas in 1950, we
had seventeen workers supporting each retiree, the number
could drop to *one* in the next century. The revenue shortfall,
they say, will be $232 billion by 2020. Life expectancy is
increasing faster than previously predicted, while the fertility
rate is falling faster than was previously thought. By 2050, the
number of retirees will reach 80 million people. The entitlement system is not sustainable, and very little, short of privatization, can avert a major collapse.

Finally, the evaluation of Henry Aaron and Robert Reis-
chauer of the Brookings Institution (*Countdown to Reform*)
corroborates much of these data but maintains that the
"Chicken Little" position is just plain wrong. Having until
2034, they say, does not amount to a crisis, and Social Security can be saved in its present form by enacting modest cuts in
benefits, levying modest tax increases, and increasing the age
of elibility for Social Security as well as taxing SS benefits like
any other pension. The problem, as the authors admit, is that
public opinion polls reveal very little support for these policies,
so the only solution is to phase them in slowly, thus triggering
less opposition.

How much trouble are we really in, then? Are we, as Joseph
Tainter maintains, rapidly reaching the point of diminishing

returns, or is this unwarranted alarmism, as Aaron and Reis-chauer suggest? As I said, I am not an economist, but here is what I conclude from my research in this area:

1. The long-range outlook is not good, as the trustees' report of the SSA freely admits.
2. We *are* becoming an older population, the fertility rate *is* dropping, and we may well reach a situation toward the end of this century in which the ratio of worker to recipient is 1:1. This will indeed require drastic measures, but as the Brookings' authors note, Americans don't want higher taxes or lower benefits, even in the case of moderate measures, let alone draconian ones.
3. One thing everybody seems to agree on is that if we want to put a positive spin on these dates (2015 and 2034), and say that we've got time to spare, we must realize that a prime factor behind this "healthy" situation is the strong economic growth that has taken place in this country since 1995. It is this in particular that is giving the entitlement situation a boost, because such growth increases revenues (payroll taxes) flowing into both Social Security and Medi-care. The only trouble is, capitalism operates in terms of ups and downs, and as the trustees' report candidly says, "we cannot prudently rely on economic growth." Nor can we reasonably project it indefinitely into the future. In short, a structural crunch does seem likely sometime in the twenty-first century.

This last point strikes me as the crucial issue. In *Gray Dawn*, Peter Peterson claims that the benefit outlays for Social Secu-rity, Medicare, Medicaid, and federal civilian and military pen-sions will exceed total federal revenues by 2030. Between

1980 and 1990, the national debt went from being 34 percent of the Gross National Product (GNP) to 59 percent of it. By 1996, the debt amounted to $5 trillion, and interest payments on this were eating up one-sixth of the national budget. I suspect that only continued economic growth can outflank this kind of debt and interest burden, and I just don't think we can count on this happening. The accuracy, then, of Tainter's thesis as it applies to America's economic future remains unclear. My own sense is that we shall be in serious trouble by mid-century.

Turning to Item (c), the collapse of American intelligence, we find a picture that is unambiguously bleak. The following data are going to seem invented; please be assured, they are not.

• Forty-two percent of American adults cannot locate Japan on a world map, and according to Garrison Keillor (National Public Radio, 22 March 1997), another survey revealed that nearly 15 percent couldn't locate the United States (!). Keillor remarked that this was like not being able to "grab your rear end with both hands," and he suggested that we stop being so assiduous, on the eve of elections, about trying to get out the vote.

• A survey taken in October 1996 revealed that one in ten voters did not know who the Republican or Democratic nominees for president were. This is particularly sobering when one remembers that one of the questions traditionally asked in psychiatric wards as part of the test for sanity is "Who is the president of the United States?"

• Very few Americans understand the degree to which corporations have taken over their lives. But according to a poll taken by *Time* magazine, nearly 70 percent of them believe in the existence of angels; and another study turned up the fact that 50 percent believe in the presence of UFOs and space aliens on earth, while a Gallup poll (reported on CNN, 19 August 1997) revealed that 71 percent believe that the U.S. government is engaged in a cover-up about the subject. More than 30 percent believe they have made contact with the dead.

• A 1995 article in the *New York Times* reported the results of a survey that revealed that 40 percent of American adults (this could be upward of 70 million people) did not know that Germany was our enemy in World War II. A Roper survey conducted in 1996 revealed that 84 percent of American college seniors couldn't say who was president at the start of the Korean War (Harry Truman). Fifty-eight percent of American high school seniors cannot understand a newspaper editorial in *any* newspaper, and a U.S. Department of Education survey of 22,000 students in 1995 revealed that 50 percent were unaware of the Cold War, and that 60 percent had no idea of how the United States came into existence.

• At one point in 1996, Jay Leno invited a number of high school students to be on his television program and asked them to complete famous quotations from major American documents, such as the Gettysburg Address and the Declaration of Independence. Their response in each case was to stare at him blankly. As a kind of follow-up, on his show of 3 June 1999, Leno screened a video of interviews he had conducted a few days before at a university graduation ceremony. He did not identify the institution in question; he told his TV audience only that the students he had interviewed included graduate students as well as undergraduates. The group included men, women, and people of color. Leno posed eight questions, as follows:

1. Who designed the first American flag?
     Answers included Susan B. Anthony (born in 1820) and "Betsy Ford."

2. What were the Thirteen Colonies free from, after the American Revolution?

    One student said, "The East Coast."

3. What was the Gettysburg Address?

    One student replied, "An address to Getty"; another said, "I don't know the exact address."

4. Who invented the lightbulb?

    Answers included Thomas Jefferson.

5. What is three squared?

    One student said, "Twenty-seven"; another said, "Six."

6. What is the boiling point of water?

    Answers included 115° F.

7. How long does it take the earth to rotate once on its axis?

    The two answers Leno received here were "Light-years" (which is a measure of distance, not time) and "Twenty-four axises [sic]."

8. How many moons does the earth have?

    The student questioned said she had taken astronomy a few years back and had gotten an A in the course but that she couldn't remember the correct answer.

It is important to note that not a single student interviewed had the correct answer to *any* of these questions. Leno's comment on this pathetic debacle says it all: "And the Chinese are stealing secrets from *us*?"

• A 1998 survey by the National Constitution Center revealed that only 41 percent of American teenagers can name the three branches of government, but 59 percent can name the Three Stooges. Only 2 percent can name the chief justice of the Supreme Court; 26 percent were unable to identify the vice president. In the early 1990s, the National Assessment of Education Progress reported that 50 percent of seventeen year olds could not express 9/100 as a percentage, and nearly 50 percent couldn't place the Civil War in the correct half century—data that the *San Antonio Express News* characterized as evidence of the "steady lobotomizing" of American culture. In another study of seventeen year olds, only 4 percent could read a bus schedule, and only 12 percent could arrange six common fractions in order of size.

• Ignorance of the most elementary scientific facts on the part of American adults is nothing less than breathtaking. In a survey conducted for the National Science Foundation in October 1995, 56 percent of those polled said that electrons were larger than atoms; 63 percent stated that the earliest human beings lived at the same time as the dinosaurs (a chronological error of more than 60 million years); 53 percent said that the earth revolves around the sun in either a day or a month (that is, only 47 percent understood that the correct answer is one year); and 91 percent were unable to state what a molecule was. A random telephone survey of more than two thousand adults, conducted by Northern Illinois University, revealed that 21 percent believed that the sun revolved around the earth, with an additional 7 percent saying that they did not know which revolved around which.

• Of the 158 countries in the United Nations, the United States ranks forty-ninth in literacy. Roughly 60 percent of the adult population has never read a book of any kind, and only 6 percent reads as much as one book *a year*, where *book* is defined to include Harlequin romances and self-help manuals. Something like 120 million adults are illiterate or read at no better than a fifth-grade level. Among readers age twenty-one to thirty-five, 67 percent regularly read a daily newspaper in 1965, as compared with 31 percent in 1998.

• In a telephone survey conducted in 1998, 12 percent of Americans, asked who the wife of the biblical Noah was, said

"Joan of Arc" (reported on National Public Radio, 13 June 1998).

•In 1997, as a hoax, the attorney general of the state of Missouri submitted a proposal to an international academic accrediting agency (not identified) to establish an institution he named Eastern Missouri Business College, which would grant Ph.D.'s in marine biology and genetic engineering, as well as in business. The faculty would include, inter alia, Moe Howard, Jerome Howard, and Larry Fine—that is, the Three Stooges; and the proposed motto on the college seal, roughly translated from the Latin, was Education Is for the Birds. The response? Academic accreditation was granted.

Now this story was reported on the radio program "Car Talk," hosted by National Public Radio, and I have no idea whether it is true. It itself could be a hoax. But what I find interesting is that I am unable to dismiss it out of hand, a priori, as a joke. In fact, it could very well be true—which ambiguity itself is a sign of the times.

•In 1998 the Massachusetts Board of Education instituted a literacy test for teachers, pegged at the level of an exam for a high school equivalency diploma. Of the eighteen hundred prospective teachers who took it, 59 percent failed. In response to this, the interim commissioner of education, one Frank Haydu III, announced that the passing grade would be lowered. The board finally reversed the decision, and the commissioner resigned. But that 59 percent of a large group of potential teachers had severe problems with high school spelling and punctuation, and that an educational administrator would declare this no obstacle to the performance of their jobs, are as good indicators as any of the twilight phase of our nation.

•In a similar vein, when the College Board, which administers the SAT exam to high school seniors applying to college, discovered that the average verbal score had dropped from 478 in 1963 to 424 in 1995 (this on a scale from 200 to 800), it "recentered" the scoring so that 424 became 500, and 730 became 800 (a perfect score).

· According to the *Wall Street Journal* (31 March 1989), only 10 percent of applicants in Chicago were able to meet the minimum literacy standard for mail-clerk jobs, and the Motorola Corporation reported that 80 percent of all applicants screened nationally failed a test of seventh-grade English and fifth-grade math.

These kinds of horror stories are multiplying in our culture at an alarming rate, and they are corroborated by the most casual observations that many of us now make on a daily basis. It is as though America has become a gigantic dolt-manufacturing machine. We now see common words misspelled on CNN, for example, or on labels in supermarkets (CAESER SALAD). Below are some personal anecdotes; I am guessing you have a list of your own.

Item: A fancy restaurant I had lunch at in Salt Lake City, bearing an elegant carved wooden sign done in Art Deco style, listing hours of operation, with the word *Sunday* spelled "S-u-n-d-y" on it—actually carved into the wood. A sign outside of a hospital clinic in Washington, D.C.: INFANT, CHILDERN & ADULT CARE.

Item: A visit I made a few years ago to several creative writing classes at a college in the Midwest, only to discover that not a single student in any of these classes had ever heard of Robert Browning, whereas I was memorizing "My Last Duchess" when I was in high school. A colleague at this same school telling me that one of his students, a twenty-year-old male, told him that he had never read a novel.

Item: The growing inability, which I have observed over nearly three decades of teaching, of the majority of undergraduate students to analyze an argument, or identify the evidence for an argument, or construct a grammatically coherent sentence. Essays turned in with sentences such as "In this paper I are going to show that . . ." My asking one student, in all innocence, what her first language was, only to be told it was English.

Item: A listing in the *Portland Oregonian* (10 April 1998), under "Literary Events": "Hear works from William Butler Yeats, Robert Frost and T. S. Eliot read allowed." (Such a notice is itself, one might venture to say, a literary event.) An announcement on National Public Radio (early in 1999) that they would be interviewing Edmund White, author of a book on Marcel "Prowst" and recipient of a "Guh-genheim" fellowship.

Item: A phone call I make to the foreign currency department of a major commercial bank because I have received a bill from Holland and need to know the guilder-dollar exchange rate. The clerk can't find a listing for Holland because, as it later turns out, it is listed as the Netherlands. "Is Holland the same as Denmark?" she asks me.

Item: I am asked to give a lecture at a southwestern university on the "crisis of American intelligence," and the talk is written up for the school newspaper by a student in her late thirties. In an article of fewer than 250 words, there are seven errors of elementary grammar and one completely incoherent sentence. (I am guessing that this was not a deliberate attempt to satirize the lecture, which would, in fact, have been wonderful.)

Item: An interview I have for a job as an editor of publications for a national higher education association. The association—I'll call it the NA—has, as part of its declared mission, "the improvement of the quality of liberal arts education." What it means by this, however, is not the preservation of any type of core curriculum or academic standards, but the moving of students toward "social action" (vaguely defined) and the acquiring of hands-on skills useful for jobs in the twenty-first century. (For this purpose, the NA receives heavy corporate funding.) In the course of the interview, I raise the issue of knowledge for its own sake, of knowing what makes oneself, and society, tick. The NA president, who is conducting the interview, stares at me for a moment and says, "Well, that's fine, if one is interested in a withdrawn or contemplative life." I say, "I don't think it necessarily leads to that." "What else would it be good for?" she asks, almost angry now. And, much in the way I might have to explain the concept to a college freshman, I reply, "Well, ideally, at least, such an education changes your sensibilities. Its aim is the transformation of the psyche. Students can then be *very* active in the world, but they have a much larger understanding of what the world is about, and how they fit into it." My interviewer nods imperceptibly; it's obvious she has no idea of what I am talking about. And I think: This woman is a leader in the field of higher education, and she has literally no idea of the deeper meaning of a liberal education. Whereas my influence on higher education is virtually nonexistent, hers is enormous. It's not that through her influence students learn to scoff at a nonutilitarian notion of a liberal education; rather, they never get to learn that such a notion even exists.

If the redistribution of wealth outlined earlier reflects a "seismic shift" in American society, a similar kind of shift can be seen in the tenor of American attitudes and intellectual abilities (nor are the two trends unrelated). Thus, for example, in an interview with Peter Coyote on National Public Radio (circa 1995), the actor matter-of-factly alluded to the great "hostility toward intelligence" that was now part of American culture. Or consider the repeated, and accurate, use of the phrase "dumbing down" in everyday discussions and in the press. The celebration of ignorance that characterizes America today can be seen in the enormous success of a film like *Forrest Gump*, in which a good-natured idiot is made into a hero; or in the immensely popular TV sitcom *Cheers*, in which intellectual interest of any sort is portrayed as phony and pretentious, whereas outright stupidity is equated with that which is warmhearted and authentic. If my colleague at Midwest U now has a student who never read a novel, how long before he has a student who asks him, "What's a novel?" (In fact, millions of Americans already don't know the difference between fiction and nonfiction.) If the students don't recognize Browning now, how long before they have never heard of Shakespeare? How long before the *New York Times* and the *Washington Post* fold for lack of subscribers, or until the English language becomes as inaccessible to the majority of Americans as Chaucer's Middle English is to them now? How long before intellectual excitement is regarded as a historical phenomenon, or a bizarre frame of mind, or just—not regarded?

In his introduction to the book *Dumbing Down: Essays on the Strip-Mining of American Culture*, John Simon notes that a whole world of learning is disappearing before our eyes, in merely one generation. We cannot expect, he says, to make a mythological allusion anymore, or use a foreign phrase, or refer to a famous historical event or literary character, and still be understood by more than a tiny handful of people. (Try this in virtually any group setting, and note the reaction. This is an excellent wake-up call as to what this culture is about, and how totally alien to it you are.) Indeed, using Lewis Lapham's

criteria for genuine literacy—having some familiarity with a min-
imal number of standard texts (Marx, Darwin, Dickens . . .),
and being able to spot irony—it may even be the case that the
number of genuinely literate adults in the United States
amounts to fewer than 5 million people—that is, less than 3
percent of the total population.

In 1953, Ray Bradbury published *Fahrenheit 451*—later
made into a movie by François Truffaut—which depicts a
future society in which intelligence has largely collapsed and
the reading of books is forbidden by law. People sit around
interacting with screens (referred to as "the family") and taking
tranquilizers. Today, nearly five decades later, isn't this largely
the point at which we have arrived? Do not the data cited
above suggest that most of our neighbors are, in fact, the mindless automatons depicted in Truffaut's film? True, the story
does contain a class of "book people" who hide in the forest
and memorize the classics, to pass on to future generations—
and this vignette does, in fact, provide a clue as to what just
might enable our civilization to eventually recover—but the
majority of citizens on the eve of the twenty-first century watch
an *average* of four hours of TV a day, pop Prozac and its deriva-
tives like candy, and perhaps read a Danielle Steel novel once
a year.

How did all of this come about? What are the causes of such
a state of affairs? "Were we this dumb before television?" asks
a character in DeLillo's *White Noise*. That's a big part of it, of
course, and it goes far beyond what Neil Postman (*Amusing
Ourselves to Death*) and many others have pointed out: that the
content of most TV programming assumes an audience of
morons. It also has something to do with a medium that creates an attention span in its viewers of about ten seconds, and
assumes that real learning can take place via images. These
problems also afflict the Internet and most microchip-driven

communication, as I shall discuss below. But following up on Items (a) and (b), from our list of factors involved in decline, an equally important issue is that the inequality of wealth and declining marginal returns on investment in complexity create a situation in which the educational system and intellectual production are negatively affected on a number of levels.

At the most immediate level, of course, is the disintegration of the public school system, and the loss of its economic base. What follows is a matter of public record. When I graduated from high school in 1962, littering the halls was considered a serious offense. Within ten years, at the very same high school, a girl was raped in broad daylight, and the situation has only escalated as the years have gone by. By the late 1980s, students bringing guns to school was a common occurrence, with the occasional student getting shot as a result, and by the late 1990s, we have been witness to frequent massacres (something like eight in a two-year period). Who could be concerned about studying the Constitution, in such a context, which now seemed a bit of a joke anyway? Teachers have effectively become baby-sitters, and they are often relieved if they can manage to get through the day without a violent incident. And if I memorized Robert Browning at age sixteen, most of today's college undergraduates have never heard of Robert Browning, and in graduate school—the only place where our youth might actually encounter the works of Browning—the students are frequently taught that such work has no intrinsic meaning and is nothing more than the cultural expression of a wealthy class of dead, white, "colonialist" males.

Even beyond this postmodern claptrap, the college/university situation in the United States has finally wound up in the position of the Church in the late Middle Ages, which sold people indulgences (read *diplomas*) so that they could get into heaven (read *a well-paying job*). This has become the rule at

thousands of institutions of higher education, where a grade
of *B* is now considered average (or slightly below), and where
A's are given out almost automatically so as not to threaten
student enrollments, on which institutional funds depend.
One of the most depressing accounts of this is Peter Sacks'
book, *Generation X Goes to College,* which documents how
higher education has been reduced to entertainment, and how
college administrators defend the students' "right" to this,
rather than the (increasingly rare) faculty members' desire to
maintain genuine academic standards. After nearly losing his
job as a result of the latter, Sacks (the author's pen name) managed to get tenure by cynically, but surreptitiously, treating his
classes like kindergarten play groups. Overnight, his previously negative student evaluations turned into raves; and to an
administration motivated only by the "bottom line," he became
a "valuable" faculty member. So he got tenure by destroying the
very education on which tenure is supposedly based, and his
own situation is hardly unique. As many faculty members have
discovered, you can provoke real hostility from students merely by presenting required course material, and many students
assume (usually, quite rightly) that administrators—who are
the actual intended audience for course evaluations—will pun-
ish professors who expect too much of them. Paul Trout, who
teaches English at Montana State University, notes that these
evaluations typically ask students to rate their instructors in
terms of "stimulation of interest" and "concern for students."
They don't ask whether the course was demanding, the work-
load challenging, the grading tough, or whether the students
learned a lot.

A similar assessment is provided by Mark Edmundson of
the University of Virginia. Writing in *Harper's* magazine in 1997,
Edmundson relates that he typically gets good teaching evalua-

tions from his students because of his classroom persona—
bland, humorous, detached. He reports that an "attitude of
calm consumer expertise . . . pervades the responses" on the
evaluation forms, and that the students have a "serene belief"
that his function is to entertain them. He says that he would
like the students to say that the course has changed their lives,
but admits that this would require a real encounter with him
or the texts, and that that would work against him. What works,
says Edmundson, is "coming across as an urbane, mildly ironic, endlessly affable guide to this intellectual territory, operating
without intensity, generous, funny, and loose." The Prozac personality, one might say. And why does this work? Precisely
because liberal education *is*, now, ineffective; because "university culture, like American culture writ large, is . . . ever more
devoted to consumption and entertainment, to the using and
using up of goods and images." The central thrust of our consumer culture, he adds, is "buy in order to be," and the culture
of the university moves within this new orbit. As a result, "the
kids are shocked if their college profs don't reflexively suck up
to them." The university's relationship with its "customers," he
says, is "nearly servile." The unstated directive, from the administration to the faculty, is this: "Teach what pulls the kids in, or
walk." And so, queries Edmundson, "What about entire departments that don't deliver? If the kids say no to Latin or Greek, is
it time to dissolve classics? Such questions are being entertained more and more seriously by university administrators."

There has been a process going on in the United States
since the 1960s, part of the whole dumbing-down phenomenon described above, that is, because of economic factors, affecting every aspect of intellectual or educational
activity. In his book *The Postmodern Condition*, Jean-François
Lyotard describes it as follows:

Knowledge in the form of an informational commodity indis-
pensable to productive power is already, and will continue to
be, a major—perhaps *the* major—stake in the worldwide
competition for power. It is conceivable that the nation-
states will one day fight for control of information, just as
they battled in the past for control over territory, and after-
wards for control of access to and exploitation of raw materials and cheap labor. A new field is opened for industrial
and commercial strategies on the one hand, and political and
military strategies on the other. . . . The nature of knowledge cannot survive unchanged within this context of general transformation. It can fit into the new channels, and
become operational, only if learning is translated into quantities of information. . . . We may thus expect a thorough
exteriorization of knowledge with respect to the "knower," at
whatever point he or she may occupy in the knowledge process. The old principle that the acquisition of knowledge is
indissociable from the training (*Bildung*) of minds, or even
of individuals, is becoming obsolete and will become even
more so. . . . Knowledge is and will be produced in order to
be sold, it is and will be consumed in order to be valorized
in a new production: in both cases, the goal is exchange.

Commodification of knowledge necessarily means a loss of
nuance, and we see this everywhere. Thus in 1959, the Strate-
meyer Syndicate in New York made a decision to dumb down
the famous Hardy Boys series, a set of books originally ghost-
written by a talented Canadian author, Leslie McFarlane. The
original versions were, given their intended audience, fairly
complex in both intellectual and emotional terms. The
rewrites, on the other hand, were stripped down to pure plot in
a kind of cops-and-robbers formula, and words that might
require looking up in a dictionary were eliminated. Any form of
emotional nuance—any passage suggesting ambiguity, uncer-

tainty, or awkwardness—was replaced by statements of bland avowal. The teenagers who were reading these books in the mid-1960s were no longer challenged by them; like so much else, the books had been reduced to mental chewing gum.

I spoke earlier of the phenomenon of economic disparity getting worse because wealthy elites are able to cash in on the very process of decline. This is no less true of the intellectual world. Kent Carroll, cofounder of the New York publishing firm Carroll & Graf, notes that publishing is now little more than brand marketing. Publishers, he says, feel no larger obligation than to give readers what they want, and that amounts to miracles and magic, the opportunity to "reinvent" themselves. This "reinvention," however, is not in the tradition of, say, Ralph Waldo Emerson—not, in short, about the good life—but is simply about self-absorption, "self-actualization." This has resulted in books that avoid confronting readers with uncomfortable truths, which they prefer not to hear; once again, a trend that is not likely to be reversed.

In this regard, it is terrifying to note that within a few short months in 1997, Books & Co., one of the last great independent bookstores in New York, had to fold; HarperCollins canceled the contracts of more than one hundred of its authors and sold Basic Books, its "intellectual" division and an academic gem; and the New York Times ran an article reporting that so-called midlist authors—those who don't write best-sellers (what I would guess amounts to more than 99 percent of American writers)—were now being heavily rejected by major publishing firms in favor of those few "stars" who could guarantee mass-market sales (John Grisham, Stephen King, etc.).

Corporate takeover of intellectual property has become quite dramatic, and it has resulted in the replacement of intelligent citizens by mindless consumers, and a corresponding conceptual flattening of public discourse. According to journalist and media expert Ben Bagdikian, whereas in 1981 twenty corporations controlled over half of the eleven thousand magazines published in the United States, by 1988 the number had dropped to three. In fact, a mere twenty-three corporations control most of the business in American newspapers, film, TV, books, and journals—firms such as Bertelsmann, General Electric, Paramount, Hearst, and Time Warner. Time Warner is now one of the largest book publishers in the world, the largest music company, and the owner of *Time*, *Life*, *People*, and the Book of the Month Club. Along with TCI, it is the owner of cablevision systems that serve 47 percent of the American cable audience, including HBO and CNN. For such firms, as one literary agent recently put it, selling books is no different from selling popcorn. When merger and monopoly drive the bottom line into becoming a matter of profit and nothing more, a collapsing level of intellectual discourse is a foregone conclusion. McWorld's takeover of the mental sphere on a global scale, says Benjamin Barber, amounts to a kind of "default totalitarianism."

We see the results of this everywhere. Campus bookstores have become largely toy stores, selling only course texts, mugs, and stuffed animals. Deans and college presidents model themselves on corporate CEOs, and they use the language, the odd doublespeak, of corporate management. (Carol Christ, provost of the University of California at Berkeley, in the Winter 1996 *Bulletin* of the Association of Departments of English, writes of "maximizing leverage for faculty positions by building on partnerships," decreasing the "investment" in graduate education, etc.) Serious authors are lucky to get their work published, as Americans are now able to read only short, sloganistic books that promise to improve their lives overnight; and the massive corporate buyout of independent publishers— for example, Bertelsmann's purchase of Random House in

1998—accelerates this trend. Hence, Bantam and Double-
day, also owned by Bertelsmann, flood the market with books
on how to get rich, live forever, or lose weight, or they spout the
latest bits of New Age "wisdom." As of this writing, most book
publishing in the United States is in the hands of six corporations, most of them foreign. All of these changes reflect a culture in which corporate profit and its associated mentality have
begun to dictate everything. After all, why read (let alone memorize) Robert Browning when the *cash* value of things is the
only value of things?

The rise of the new microchip technology, a major player in
the new economic order, also contributes heavily to the dumbing down of America and the commodification of knowledge.
In *The Gutenberg Elegies*, Sven Birkerts faults the Internet and
the advent of hypertext for disrupting the "vertical" experience
provided by the printed word. The experience of sitting with a
book, he says, enables the reader to sink into a private world
and ultimately discover who he or she is. There is a process of
matching your own emotions against those of the protagonist
in a novel, for example, whereby you can get a deeper sense of
your self. What hypertext provides, in contrast, is a "horizontal"
experience of skimming across related (or, for that matter,
unrelated) ideas, opening up kaleidoscopic windows, as it
were. The medium works against depth and self-reflection,
and the net effect (no pun intended) is a diffuse self, an identity that is finally forged by a kind of meaningless infotainment.
There is no context here, and indeed, most of Generation X
lacks all sense of history or cultural continuity. Increasingly, we
live in a "weightless order" in which all information is equally
significant. Subjective space evaporates, to be replaced by
mental theme parks that assist in the process of moving our
culture from wisdom to schlock. "Language," writes Birkerts,
"is the soul's ozone layer, and we thin it at our peril."

Finally, we come to the phenomenon of postmodernism and deconstruction, a philosophical viewpoint that seems to have taken over much of the academy, and which has become part of the air we breathe: the notion that nothing is absolute, that one value is as good as another, that there is no difference between knowledge and opinion, and that any text or set of ideas is merely a mask for someone's political agenda. This lends itself well to the new world of microchip technology, inasmuch as it promotes a valueless universe; it is also a great way to hide from the real social and economic problems discussed above. A philosophy of despair masquerading as radical intellectual chic, postmodernism is, in fact, the ideological counterpart to the civilizational collapse that is going on around us; or, as cultural critic Fredric Jameson has written, the "cultural logic of late capitalism," in which the entire world is turned into a shopping mall. A good description of it is provided by Robert Grudin in his novel *Book*, in which a university professor named Giorgio Mufeta (the Italian word *muffa* means "mildew")

> eloquently painted [in his lectures] an amoral, asymetrical human world, barren of esthetic meaning and substantive only in terms of power patterns which, like ever-changing electrical fields, played across its face. This vertiginous cosmos allowed of no solid meaning or knowledge. Beauty, wisdom and order were empty rationalizations. Love, sympathy and trust were vulgar buzz-words. Competition reigned supreme, and the best competitors were those who could understand and exploit the then-dominant patterns of power.
>
> The literary implications of this worldview were quite simple. Literature had no implicit human meaning at all. Literature meant what people interpreted it to mean, or what people could convince others that it meant. And this cyni-

cal canon applied not only to modern literature but to the so-called classics. Plato, Dante, Shakespeare: These were no longer corpora to be studied with appreciative attention. Rather they were like empty palaces, ripe for occupation by militant forces of interpretation.

One does not have to restrict oneself to fiction to find descriptions of this new professorial class. In a very balanced and sensitive memoir, *In Plato's Cave*, Alvin Kernan, who taught English at Yale and Princeton for many years, describes the "tectonic shift" that took place in the academy over the course of his professional career. His own raison d'être was something that the academy now views as a bit hoary: "I was one of those," he writes, "who feel that the most satisfactory end in life is knowledge; not money or power or prestige, but an understanding of people and the world they inhabit." The old university, prior to postmodernism and political correctness, entertained Enlightenment goals that energized it. The intellectual enterprise was an exciting one, because faculty members believed that it was possible to construct a total model of society, and of human life, and that freedom lay in this direction. All this is gone now, says Kernan; postmodernism brought to the table not merely the denial of truth but also the denial of the *ideal* of truth. Facts are now regarded as a "fetish," all methodology is "problematic," and sometimes even the highest forms of culture are despised. When feminists—in this case, Susan McClary—can say that Beethoven's Ninth Symphony is filled with "the throttling, murderous rage of a rapist incapable of attaining release," we see how nakedly sick the deconstructive enterprise finally is. This is not merely intellectual failure; it is moral failure as well.

And yet, as Kernan admits, this is not the whole story. Postmodernism's legacy is going to be a complex one, for within limits, the deconstructionists were right. Texts *do* lend themselves to more than one interpretation; the concerns of women and minorities *had* been excluded from critical consideration; artistic and intellectual achievements *do* emerge in political contexts; and much of what we live with is, in fact, socially constructed. The problem arises when this position is pushed to the limit, such that you abandon the search for truth and even deny it exists, repudiate the reality of history and intellectual tradition, and claim that everything is a "text," without any intrinsic meaning or referent. This is nothing short of nihilism; and during Kernan's lifetime, the search for truth was replaced, as far as personnel were concerned, by "teaching and publication as careerism and political action." "Once hating culture becomes cultural in itself," comments the French philosopher Alain Finkielkraut, "the life of the mind loses all significance." Or as Alexis de Tocqueville once put it, "When the past no longer illuminates the future, the spirit walks in darkness."

This brings us to Item (d) on our list, spiritual death, which naturally overlaps with the collapse of mental abilities, but which is much larger than this, encompassing the phenomena of white noise and Bostock Nation referred to in the Introduction. It is, however, difficult to see this from within the culture itself. As Marshall McLuhan once pointed out, if you could ask a fish what was the most obvious feature of its environment, probably the last thing it would say would be "water." If you swim in it all the time, you just don't notice it; this is how any culture functions. What is crucial, of course, is the nature of the water.

In the case of the United States, the "water" is corporate consumerism. It functions as a kind of "skin" that covers everything, like an all-encompassing mantle—a total environment,

as it were. (Calvin Coolidge: "The business of America is business.") This is our ethos, our civilizational essence. This mental toxicity permeates every part of our landscape, and if you
can just stand back for a moment and look, it appears in clear
detail: the fact that most "news" is actually business news; the
constant stream of "cold calls" you get from various companies asking you whether you want to change your long-distance
carrier, or have a chip in your windshield removed, or obtain a
lower rate on your mortgage; the public perception of the president not as a statesman but as, in effect, a corporate CEO; the
pursuit of shopping as entertainment for 98 percent of the
population, which never thinks that there might be something
wrong with this. "There is barely an empty space in our culture," writes social critic James Twitchell, "not already carrying
commercial messages." Or as George Steiner once put it, we
live in a "systematic suppression of silence."

One effect of this commercial domination of our lives is the
pervasiveness of kitsch, or hype, as part of our collective spiritual death. In his book *BAD, or the Dumbing of America*, Paul
Fussell defines kitsch as "something phony, clumsy, witless,
untalented, vacant, or boring that many Americans can be per-
suaded is genuine, graceful, bright, or fascinating." He cites
Lawrence Welk and George Bush as obvious examples, but
this is the tip of the iceberg, for the truth is that kitsch *is* our
culture. In the United States, writes Fussell, "nothing will
thrive unless inflated by hyperbole and gilded with a fine coat
of fraud." One sees this everywhere, because in the din of the
cultural noise, one has to gloss up an idea, package it in a
sound bite or flashy formula, in order for it to get a hearing at
all. (This is true even if one is attacking the sound-bite culture
itself.) Content doesn't really matter, because it is always the
same: Slogans work; hype is life. Virtual reality is not merely a
cyberphenomenon, in short; rather, it defines the medium in

which we swim, and from within this culture, there is no escape. The "mind" of the twenty-first century, for most people, will be a weird hybrid of Bill Gates and Walt Disney, as so-called cyberpunk novelists such as William Gibson (*Neuromancer*) or Neal Stephenson (*Snow Crash*) have already recognized. We live in a collective adrenaline rush, a world of endless promotional/commercial bullshit that masks a deep systemic emptiness, the spiritual equivalent of asthma.

This phenomenon of the "skin" of mass consumerism shows up everywhere, for we have become a nation unable to think *except* by means of slogans. A few books are published on "incest survivors," and overnight, hundreds of thousands of women discover that this is what they are (and some, of course, *are*). Men go to "men's workshops" and cry, because they are told they must learn to become sensitive. Joseph Campbell, whose understanding of mythology was woefully inadequate from an anthropological standpoint, tells TV viewers to "follow your bliss," and this becomes their life theme, as they remain blissfully unaware of the fact that real spirituality is most often a working *against* the grain. "Consciousness" gurus declare that we are in the midst of a "paradigm shift," and millions, who never managed to understand the *present* paradigm, grunt the phrase like a mantra. Each year (or, sometimes, month) there is a new slogan to get jazzed up about, taken to an extreme, and then summarily dropped for the *next* exciting new slogan that comes along. "Thinking" now means nothing more than wandering through the latest mental theme park.

The inevitable result of all this is the inability of the American public to distinguish garbage from quality; in fact, as Paul Fussell points out, they identify garbage *as* quality. Thus, for example, the rise of a huge New Age industry, immensely successful financially, and based on the premise that your rational mind is your worst enemy. The rubbish content of this stuff, such as *Mutant Message Down Under* or *The Celestine Prophecy*, is phenomenal, and sales are in direct proportion to it. Robert Fulghum, a former Seattle high school teacher who told his readers that history should be replaced by myth and that everything they needed to know in life they learned in kindergarten, was at least completely candid about the source of his success, stating that his books were popular because people were searching for simple answers to complex problems. An equivalent phenomenon is Deepak Chopra, who publishes books with titles such as *Escaping the Prison of the Intellect*. On one level, he has a point, in that we can get caught up in cognitive categories, to the detriment of reality. All well and good. The problem is that Chopra seems to be addressing an audience that for the most part hasn't managed to find its way into the "prison of the intellect" in the *first* place. It is one thing to see the limits of the Enlightenment tradition after you have studied it for a few decades. It's another to reject it before you have ever been exposed to it. Some time ago, Bruce Barcott, a Seattle writer and reporter, attended one of Chopra's workshops, which typically draw huge crowds, and took notes for three days. He then wrote an article describing the event, relating how, when he got home and read over his notes, he discovered that they consisted of empty platitudes. It is perhaps striking that in a room of several hundred people, this reporter may have been the only individual not sitting there in a state of rapt adoration, regarding the platitudes as profundities. More troublesome, to my mind, is the fact that Chopra's New Age philosophy gets dignified by being aired on PBS—the "educational" channel (which subsequently lionized Suze Orman on how to get rich); or that in the spring of 1997, Arnold Schwarzenegger is awarded an honorary degree by the University of Wisconsin–Superior, and Oprah Winfrey is asked to deliver the commencement address at Wellesley(!).

It is also the case that New Age inanities, as well as various other myths and historical falsifications, get published by the large commercial publishing firms because they are guaranteed to sell, whereas books that debunk such myths, or are based on careful scholarship, can get published only by university presses (if at all), which accounted for 0.77 percent of the number of books sold in the United States in 1998. This effectively amounts to a new form of censorship, Benjamin Barber's "default totalitarianism." "The challenging writer," writes Sven Birkerts,

> is archaic—she goes begging for a publisher, and when she finds one goes begging for attention. Difficult books have always depended on loyal coteries, but as these have dwindled we find publishers less and less willing to take a chance. . . . If literature survives at all, it is as a retreat for those who refuse to assimilate to American mass culture.

As William Leach shows in *Land of Desire*, the New Age phenomenon, and its tight integration with consumer capitalism, is hardly a child of the 1970s. Mind Cure and New Thought, as it was then called, arose naturally as part of the commercial developments of the 1890s and after, for their so-called spiritual message—that people can completely shape their destinies and find total happiness—is really an economic one. To the proto–New Age groups of the early twentieth century, poverty and injustice existed only in the mind, and business magazines were quick to pick up the New Thought slogans. "No Worry" dolls were marketed by the truckload; swamis of various sorts overran the country; businessmen took yoga classes. Theodore Dreiser observed how neatly this new "religious" perspective interlocked with the new world of money and greed. The same, of course, has been true of the New Age movements of the 1970s and beyond.

All of this may, in fact, have a strange parallel with the process of evolution and natural selection. Harvard biologist Steven Jay Gould has argued that our species is a branch on the evolutionary tree that is here only against extreme odds. That branch could have easily been bypassed, he says, fallen dead, and it avoided this fate thousands of times by the merest chance. Bacteria and cockroaches, he suggests, will be here long after we are gone.

Now apply this to *cultural* evolution, and what would seem to be the rule is not the survival of the fittest, but of the slickest. How precarious real intelligence is in the world of Oprah & Chopra, in a world where the dumb and the titillating have become the standard of value! David Denby, in a discussion of Darwin's work in *The New Yorker* in 1997, asks whether things such as individualism, taste, and judgment can survive in the current American environment, for it is schlock that is adaptive, and that for which the culture selects. "Celebrity," he writes, "—even buffoonery and shamelessness—[is] the new peacock tail." This is Spengler's classical phase with a vengeance, the merger of natural selection with Gresham's Law (bad coinage drives good coinage out of circulation). PBS, after all, is hardly embarrassed by their superficial programming; they think it's hip.

One further aspect of our current spiritual collapse is our increasing inability to relate to one another with a minimum of courtesy or even awareness. It has become common now not to respond to any sort of request if the answer is no. Increasingly, if someone applies for a job and fails to get it, they are not notified to that effect; they never hear anything at all. People are also fired indirectly, with companies refusing to let them know why. We have stopped holding doors for one another; don't bother to answer messages; disappear from each other's lives without explanation or regret; betray one another and then refuse to discuss it. Rudeness is now acceptable, because I am the only one who inhabits my solipsistic world. (The flip side of this phenomenon is the replacement of civility by corporate politeness: "Have a nice day," "Thank you for choosing AT&T," etc.) At root, there is a fear of any kind of involvement at all, for real friendships require risk and vulnerability, and more and more Americans feel that they lack the psychological strength for that. Bottled rage and resentment are the norm, as millions live in isolation, without any form of community, and are content to have soap-opera characters for "friends." In this regard, I found it very revealing that by 1996, academic conferences began to be held on the "erosion of civility"—something that was unheard of even five years before that. And the extreme dark end of the spectrum here is represented by the high school massacre in Littleton, Colorado, on 20 April 1999 (Hitler's birthday, symbolically enough), when two badly alienated teenagers in black trench coats set about murdering their fellow students.

Yet another distinctive aspect of the process of spiritual death in the late twentieth century has been the collapse of the Freudian superego, that part of the mind that seeks to maintain adult behavior, social norms and standards. Of course, the superego can be very harsh and repressive, and in many ways the events of the 1960s were an attempt on the part of the id, the unconscious and instinctive part of the mind, to assert the values of naturalness and spontaneity. All well and good—we surely needed it. But despite the Reagan years and the reaction to the sixties, what is left over from that period of rebellion is a widespread refusal to grow up: infantilism as an ideology. As Peter Sacks shows (in *Generation X Goes to College*), there is very little tolerance on the part of students for any real work; "no pain, no gain" is not part of their emotional vocabulary. All that counts are my feelings, my (fragile) self-esteem, and I expect my teachers to cater to my sensitivity. Real education—apprenticing oneself to a craftsman (intellectual or otherwise)—is now regarded as elitist and authoritarian. God forbid that a student might be told that his work is of poor quality! But as long as we regard *elitism* as a dirty word, and the superego as unadulterated repression, we cannot maintain a civilization; we can only watch it come apart.

It was this conflict of values, I believe, that lay at the heart of the impeachment and subsequent trial of President Clinton in 1998–99; and while my sympathies are hardly with the Republicans here, I can appreciate their rage at a man for whom political life represented nothing more than whatever you could get away with. Writers such as Judy Mann (*Washington Post*) and Michael Oreskes (*New York Times*), who can hardly be lumped in with the self-righteous right-wing moralizers of the GOP, nevertheless saw a connection between Clinton's personality structure and the decline of the American republic. Thus, in his review of the instant best-seller *Monica's Story*, Oreskes wrote, "For those who argue that American culture is collapsing in on itself, hollowed out by self-indulgence and narcissism, 'Monica's Story' will be an original source document." As for Ms. Mann, her list of "proofs of our decline" included the observations that "our schools are a disgrace," "our culture is a joke," and that "our chief executive is . . . a blackguard." But *blackguard*, that quaint old word from a more responsible era, doesn't quite capture it; William Jefferson Clinton can be more properly described as a postmodern adolescent. In an astute comparison of Clinton and his fellow Democrat Senator Daniel Moynihan, political analyst Jeffrey Toobin highlights the difference between modern and postmodern sensibilities in no uncertain terms. Whereas Clinton told us how quickly we were going to recover our preeminence in math and science education, for example, Moynihan brought forth the data to show that this was delusional, an attitude of "if I wish it to be so, it will be." The same is true for Clinton's attempts at health-care reform, which was more about PR than about careful policy planning—a "New Age affectation," says Toobin. The major difference between the two men, according to Toobin, is that for Clinton, the notion of "character" is defined "by a kind of free-floating empathy that exists to validate feelings (feelings that may or may not have any basis in fact)," whereas in Moynihan's worldview, "character is based on intellectual integrity, on describing the world as it is, regardless of the political consequences." Moynihan, quite obviously, has a superego. For a postmodern adolescent, on the other hand, life is merely a question of whatever is popular. I fear we shall see fewer Moynihans and more Clintons in public office during the next few decades, as American civilization continues to unravel.

The merger of adolescent attitudes and corporate values can also be seen in our most prominent art form—namely, film. As movies have turned into a system of publicity and commerce, writes David Denby, they have become less interested in exploring emotional (let alone intellectual) messages. The goal, rather, is to create a sense of physical excitement. More and more, films are spectacular, violent, and impersonal, filled with "a rush of frenetic images." The context is one of corporate cynicism, in which manufactured raves are supplied to the critics in advance by the publicity people. The mass audiences view these Hollywood-formula products not at individual theaters, says Denby, "but at malls and twelveplexes, among the video games and roller rinks, where they absorb the quick-turnover attitude toward merchandise which mall life imposes on everyone." Not only are such audiences hungry for consumer "culture" and physical sensation, and totally uninterested in artistic quality, but serious film critics have less and less to say because they "can no longer appeal to a commonly held set of values"—unless mere titillation is to be regarded as a value. Thus, David Rieff rightly refers to "the startling rapidity with which the United States is becoming if not a culture-free zone then at least a place in which the arts and humanities count for little compared with commerce, the entertainment industry, and therapy. . . ."

In general, the way the commodity culture defends itself against these kinds of critiques is to label them "elitist," and argue that the commercialization of culture is a positive thing, part of a democratization process that "lets everybody in." (Personally, when someone calls me an elitist, I say thank you. It amazes me that Americans are quick to call intellectuals—who have no power at all—"elitist," yet remain oblivious to the real oligarchic elites, which are corporate. Can you imagine, in this country, a TV program along the lines of *Cheers* that ridiculed wealth instead of intelligence?) This is a mass culture, the argument goes, one that doesn't just cater to wealthy WASPs. The problem is, exactly what is this "everybody" being let in *to*? In the 1830s, Alexis de Tocqueville feared that the American experiment would result in an "egalitarian dismissal of excellence," and much later, Hannah Arendt pointed out that mass culture was not culture, but entertainment, and that to believe that a society could become cultured via this process was a fatal mistake. The expression "dumbing down" means just that. This so-called democratization is not an attempt to get the less able to stretch themselves a bit; rather, it is a reduction of everything to the lowest common denominator and the regarding of that as some kind of political triumph. We have to remember, as social critic Wendy Kaminer puts it, that "a concern for literacy and critical thinking is only democratic." The point—as Tocqueville effectively said—is that a society cannot function if nearly everyone in it is stupid, or trained to be. Instead of attacking quality for being quality, our goal should be that of Lyotard, as already cited: elitism for every-body. Dumbing down is the formula of a doomed society, not a vital one. We need to be unrepentant elitists, then; the problem is, who is "we"? Who, in thirty years, will be *left*? For every intelligent book you, the reader, might read, millions of other readers occupy themselves with titles such as *Aliens Are Among Us!* or *Protect Yourself from Emotional Abuse*, and that is, if they read at all. This situation led David Remnick, now editor of *The New Yorker,* to wonder whether there would be any readers in the future. "Not just readers of the sports pages," he wrote,

> and the jumble of self-help best-sellers and the consultant's confessions, no, but passionate readers who ignore the phone and the TV for a few hours to engage a book whose "difficulty" is that it fails to soothe the ego or flatter a limit-ed intelligence; the reader who honestly believes that the best and the deepest of what we are is on the shelf, and that to read across the shelf changes the self, changes *you*.

Don DeLillo echoes this sentiment when he writes, "If seri-ous reading dwindles to nothingness, it will probably mean that the thing we're talking about when we use the word 'identity' has reached an end."

What does all of this amount to? As I suggested in the Intro-duction, the historical process we are witness to is a convolut-ed one, because if all of this points to civilizational collapse, it is a strangely energetic kind of collapse. Money and vitality and new enterprise circulate in American culture at an astonishing speed, and if a handful of so-called elitists want to point out that it's mostly kitsch and hype, what's that to Wall Street,

Madison Avenue, and the crowds at the cineplex? As I said before, the meaning of *collapse* is in the eye of the beholder, at least in a situation such as this one. One could, in other words, argue that in the case of ancient Rome, the collapse really did *look* like a collapse. In our own case, however, it looks like a kind of renewal, and in terms of the overall globalization process—what John Gray at the London School of Economics calls a "false dawn"—what we are seeing can perhaps be more accurately described as a large-scale transformation. The question, of course, is transformation to *what?* A superficial vitality is hardly the same thing as a healthy culture; a false dawn is not a real one.

The best case I have read for the curious and problematic nature of the current cultural transformation is that of Robert Kaplan in an essay entitled "Was Democracy Just a Moment?" published in the *Atlantic Monthly* in December 1997. Kaplan points out that a world government is now emerging, one of international corporations and markets, and that this is happening "quietly and organically, the way vast developments in history take place." Of the world's one hundred largest economies, he says, fifty-one are corporations rather than countries, and the five hundred largest corporations account for 70 percent of world trade. This dense "ganglion" is the real arbiter of power, worldwide. "Corporations," writes Kaplan, "are like the feudal domains that evolved into nation-states; they are nothing less than the vanguard of a new Darwinian organization of politics . . . the forefront of real globalization." The future social landscape can already be seen in cities such as St. Louis or Atlanta, which are corporate enclaves dedicated to global business. Indeed, they don't seem to be cities at all, but collections of "hotels and corporate offices with generic architecture, 'nostalgic' tourist bubbles, zoned suburbs, and bleak urban wastelands. . . ." Kaplan quotes urban affairs expert Dennis Judd, who claims that "life within some sort of corporation is what the future will increasingly be about." As communities become "liberated" from geography, says Kaplan, as specific territory becomes politically meaningless, democracy perforce must fall apart. We are, he adds, in a phase of historical transition that will last a century or more, and when this globalization process is over, so will civil society be. As this process rolls out, "the masses become more indifferent and the elite less accountable," and the (increasingly shrinking) middle class spends its money on lotteries, health clubs, and antidepressant drugs. Spectator sports provide mass diversion, while a new form of professional combat, called "extreme fighting," is attracting sellout crowds eager to see blood. "The mood of the Colosseum," writes Kaplan, "goes together with the age of the corporation, which offers entertainment in place of values." As in the case of Rome, we are drifting toward a society comprised of an elite with little loyalty to the state, and a servile populace content with some equivalent of bread and circuses. Ted Hughes, the late poet laureate of England, drew a deliberate comparison between Rome in the early first century A.D. and our own era when he wrote, in *Tales from Ovid*, "For all its Augustan stability, [the Roman Empire] was at sea in hysteria and despair, at one extreme wallowing in the bottomless appetites and sufferings of the gladiatorial arena, and at the other searching . . . for a spiritual transcendence. . . ." Democratic elections are meaningless in such a world; politics will instead be determined by relations of power and the demeanor of society.

So the American transformation is part of a broader world-system transformation. If the twentieth century was the "American century," the twenty-first will be the "Americanized century." The ideological counterpart to this massive socioeconomic shift is the "skin" described above, the total commercial environment that circumscribes an entire mental world. A citizen will not really be a citizen in the sense that this word has always meant, and whatever he is, he will be only too happy to be offered entertainment (or "transcendence") in place of values.

As Kaplan points out, however, there is a disturbing feedback loop in this system. If we are bending the Third World to corporate ends, we won't escape from the process unscathed. From a world economy based on the ability to process large quantities of information, new forms of social stratification will emerge, and with them will come a certain form of politics, the "hybrid" regimes of the Third World, blending democratic shadow with oligarchic/authoritarian substance—but now not restricted to the Third World. Indeed, this will be the grimmest aspect of our own "classical" phase, in which the banner we wave will say DEMOCRACY, but the actual content may be precisely the four aspects of collapse outlined in this chapter. In other words, it may turn out that global-democratic-consumer culture is *defined* by acute social and economic inequality, declining marginal returns, and spiritual-intellectual disintegration; and that whereas these factors previously signaled cultural decline, they are now the pillars of a new, transnational corporate culture whose very vacuity *is* its dynamism. Politically speaking, says Kaplan, "the future of the Third World may finally be our own."

What will this look like? In *An Empire Wilderness*, Kaplan gives us a glimpse through the eyes of Cayce Boone, a Navajo who works for a local cable TV company in Tucson. Boone tells him:

> Look all around you in the Southwest; most of the buildings you see are mobile homes. Inside most of these homes are filthy people who can't read, who don't talk to each other,

who have few or no relatives or friends, who are one unpaid bill or one small tragedy away from being homeless; people who can't put food on the table or watch over their kids. The little money they have is used to install cable TV. I know. I go into these places every day. . . . When I think of the future of the United States, I think of a little girl I saw inside one mobile home, a girl who—I can tell you from my own experience—is not so untypical. She's about three years old. Her parents plop her down all day by the TV, turned to the channel for soap operas and game shows. There's dirt all over the house. There are tabloid magazines and TV schedules and beer cans. There's not much furniture, no books. It smells.

Riding on a Greyhound bus in New Mexico, Kaplan has an experience that I have also had: No one is carrying a book, or even a tabloid newspaper, and when you eavesdrop on conversations, the speech is almost incomprehensible. All of this is indicative of our future Third World status, for democracy has traditionally depended on the existence of high literacy, a large middle class, and a flexible hierarchy. But these are going under, and what is emerging is "a wilderness of region-states and suburban oases linked to a global marketplace."

One does not, of course, have to visit trailer parks in Arizona to see the assault on the human spirit. I saw it several times a week in the inner-city charter school I mentioned in the Introduction. Many of the students move in a kind of fog that is almost impossible to describe; you have to see it to understand what I am talking about. It would be easy to think that these kids are lazy, or dumb, but, for the most part, that is not what is going on. Rather, they have been robbed of their motivation, and therefore of their identity. I came away with a deep respect for the energy they *had* been able to retain, given the context of an oppressed subculture of poverty, drugs, violence, and family incarceration. When I asked one girl to define *concurrent* (we were working on vocabulary), she said, "Like in jail terms." Another student wrote a short story (one page) about working as a cook in a restaurant and roasting his classmates in an oven. In another case, I was able to locate the only source of energy a sixteen-year-old girl had—we were doing a written autobiographical exercise—when she was willing to reveal that she had been jailed the previous year for beating another girl half to death. The reason? The girl had insulted her cousin several months before.

Living at this level of survival, rage, and emotional immediacy, these students had no interest left over for any serious study; it was abstract, meant absolutely nothing to them. The flip side of the anger was the fog I referred to, a kind of sleepy, out-of-it quality that they seemed to carry around with them like an aura, and which I believe was depression. Homework rarely got done, because they never heard the teacher assign it. If the instructor said, "Take out your reading assignment," they would proceed to riffle through a large, sloppy binder that was basically a random junk pile, and not be able to find anything. Care, attention, and ambition were foreign concepts because there was no meaningful social context for such notions to exist, and no consequent motivation. Motivation is about energy, and it is the one thing you ultimately can't give someone else. If a student feels he has no future, then he has no energy, because there is no place for his immediate interests to expand. The result is an ambience that can best be described as blurry. At least half the students who were sent to me for tutoring preferred to have the lamp on my desk off rather than on, and they much preferred to sleep or zone out rather than read or think. This does not, quite obviously, describe the entire population of African-American teenagers, but it remains a reality nonetheless. As Shelby Steele puts it in *The Content of Our Character*, "the majority of blacks— those not yet in the middle class—are further behind whites today than before the victories of the civil rights movement." "The black underclass," he adds, "continues to expand rather than shrink."

We do not hear about any of this in rosy State of the Union addresses that, in effect, rave about the prosperity of the rich; and we need to be very clear about what the other end of the social spectrum is up to. In an article in the *San Francisco Chronicle* of 20 October 1985, David Lampert, himself a graduate of Stanford University's Graduate School of Business, described the "hidden curriculum" of the school as "the subconscious destruction of democratic values." The school's "ethics" course, B295, is (or was then) a training in how to outflank any external forces attempting to limit managerial autonomy—things such as constitutional entitlements, property, civil rights, and so on. The course teaches the future business elite "how to stonewall the media, how to present oneself on television and protect corporate interests, [and] how to manipulate the public and Congress. . . ." Student papers on issues such as the Love Canal come back with comments such as, "Why didn't you advise Hooker Chemical to sue the journalists who exposed the story?" while an exam question in another course states, "Assume that the memorandum you are writing will be burned before it reaches the Anti-Trust Division of the Department of Justice."

What is to be done? Lenin's answer to this question was to kill these jokers in tailored suits who are literally murdering our communities. As they build financial capital, they destroy cultural capital, human capital—the true assets of a nation. The problem—since the dilemma is structural—is that there are plenty of *other* such entrepreneurs in the wings, ready to replace them. No, something much more long-range is needed at this point.

In the case of the twilight phase of Rome, there was a monastic "class"—a tiny handful of individuals—who saw that they could not reverse these trends but that they could do their best to preserve the treasures of their civilization, the ways of thinking and living that might be appreciated in another, healthier era. And there is a potential for that today, because the very existence of the sort of writers I cite in this chapter, for example—folks such as David Denby, or Lewis Lapham, or Don DeLillo—indicates that real resistance to the New World Order is possible. Nor should we be unclear about what the treasures of our own civilization are; all we need to do is invert the factors of collapse. If social inequality is on the rise, for example, then the attempt to close the gap between rich and poor—the socialist tradition—is one of our greatest treasures. If corporate values are turning our citizens into mindless con-sumers, then the healthy "elitist" intellectual tradition of our civilization—history, philosophy, literature—is another trea-sure we have to fight for, and hand down. If the masses zone out on *Titanic* and *Wayne's World* at the cineplex, there is the whole world of Truffaut and Kurosawa, which could conceiv-ably inspire a new generation of filmmakers and moviegoers. For every jackass of a dean who is ecstatic about "distance learning" and who makes no distinction between higher edu-cation and marketing, there are a very few faculty members willing to stand up to her and tell her that there is no substitute for direct personal involvement and painstaking intellectual apprenticeship. The way of life suggested by the monastic option may attract only a minute percentage of the American population, but I believe that the potential for cultural renewal, for a dawn that this may ultimately engender, is real, and that the rewards of a life lived in terms of quality, as opposed to kitsch, are enormous.

More on all this later. What I wish to do now is consider the case of Rome, and the role of the monastic class in the transformation of the empire's fall into the rise of a new Europe.

THE MONASTIC OPTION

Lo! thy dread Empire, Chaos! is restor'd;
Light dies before thy uncreating word:
Thy hand, great Anarch! lets the curtain fall;
And Universal Darkness buries All.
                                        —Alexander Pope,
                                        The Dunciad

It would, of course, be difficult to demonstrate that the four factors discussed in the previous chapter—social inequality, increasing loss of entitlements, decreasing intellectual abilities, and spiritual death—are *causing* the collapse of American civilization. We won't know that until after the fact, and even then we won't know it—any more than we know precisely what caused the fall of Rome. Historians are still debating the latter issue fifteen hundred years later. The cause of Rome's fall remains elusive, and, of course, there was no single cause. The eminent British historian J. B. Bury held that the gradual disintegration of Rome was the result of a series of contingent events, and that does seem to be the consensus on the subject. What is likely to be true, then, is that the four factors cited previously are inevitable components of a civilization's deterioration and transformation; and this certainly was true in the case of Rome.

Consider, for example, the matter of social inequality. What we have in the case of Rome, writes the historian Meyer Reinhold, is "the impoverishment of the masses by an economic system which enriched a small propertied minority." From the time of Augustus (reigned 27 B.C.–A.D. 14), the leading economic development in the Roman Empire was the "steady concentration of land in fewer and fewer hands, with the gradual disappearance of small independent peasant landowners." The economic system was frail; it could support only a tiny minority, "whose prosperity rested on intensive exploitation of the masses living on a bare subsistence level."

It is interesting, in this regard, that whereas the Western Empire went under, the Eastern sector endured as Byzantine civilization for a very long time. The key difference was a more equitable distribution of wealth. In the East, much more of the land was owned by peasant proprietors than in the West, and therefore a correspondingly larger proportion of the total agricultural yield went to them. And in the West, but not in the East, the landed aristocracy had a stranglehold on government administration and used its power and connections to funnel cash into its own coffers, creating a class of idle rich. Not much credence, then, can be given to the theory that the Western Empire fell because of barbarian invasions, for the empire was structurally flawed in the extreme by the third century. As Michael Grant points out (in *The Fall of the Roman Empire*), the pattern was for the richest noblemen to become dramatically richer, such that the situation was, by the fifth century, grotesque. The taxes levied to maintain the army were massive, and they fell largely on the poor; but the Roman rulers also managed to ruin the middle class, which had been the backbone of the empire. It was this class, says Grant, that had held the culture of the ancient world together, and by the fourth century, it was going under. By the fifth century, it was gone, and it did not reappear in Italy until the rise of the mercantile families of the High Middle Ages.

Turning to the factor of declining marginal returns, Joseph Tainter once again does a good job of showing how nonviable Rome's policy of geographic and military expansion, which worked initially, eventually became. By the third century, nearly every denarius collected in taxes was going into military and administrative maintenance, to the point that the state was drifting toward bankruptcy. The denarius, which had a silver content of 92 percent in Nero's reign (A.D. 54–68), was down to 43 percent silver by the early third century. The third century saw even greater increases in the size of the army and the government bureaucracy, followed by further debasement of the coinage and enormous inflation. The standing army rose from 300,000 troops in A.D. 235 to about 600,000 a mere seventy years later. Investment in complexity was not merely not paying off but also bleeding the state dry. By the time the fifth century rolled around, Rome was an empire in name only.

Spiritual and intellectual collapse were unavoidable in such a demoralized context, especially because the economic life of the cities was virtually destroyed. For centuries, the aim had been to hellenize or romanize the rest of the population—to pass on the learning and ideals of Greco-Roman civilization. But as the economic crisis deepened, a new mentality arose among the masses, one based on religion, which was hostile to the achievements of higher culture. In addition, as in contemporary America, the new "intellectual" efforts were designed to cater to the masses, until intellectual life was brought down to the lowest common denominator. This, according to the great historian of Rome, M. I. Rostovtzeff, was the most conspicuous feature in the development of the ancient world during the imperial age: primitive forms of life finally drowning out the higher ones. For the truth is that civilization is impossible without a hierarchy of quality, and as soon as that gets flattened into a mass phenomenon, its days are numbered. "The main phenomenon which underlies the process of decline," wrote Rostovtzeff, "is the gradual absorption of the educated classes by the masses and the consequent simplification of all the functions of political, social, economic, and intellectual life, which we call the barbarization of the ancient world."

Religion played a critical role in these developments. By the third century, if not before, there was an attitude among many Christians that education was not relevant to salvation, and that ignorance had a positive spiritual value (an early version of *Forrest Gump*, one might say). The third century saw a sharp increase in mysticism and a belief in knowledge by revelation. Charles Radding, in *A World Made by Men*, argues that the cognitive ability of comparing different viewpoints or perspectives (quite evident in Augustine's *Confessions*, for example) had disappeared by the sixth century. Even by the fourth century, he says, what little that had survived from Greek and Roman philosophy was confused with magic and superstition (much as we see in today's New Age beliefs or in the so-called Philosophy section of many bookstores). In fact, the study of Greek—and therefore of science and philosophy—was completely abandoned. By the sixth century, the dominant mentality was superstitious, as people now lacked the capacity to manipulate abstractions logically. When Boethius published his works on philosophy, contemporaries assumed they were about the occult sciences, and he was accused of being an astrologer and magician. Thus in *The Demon-Haunted World*, Carl Sagan comments on the loss of knowledge of anatomy and surgery during this time and the corresponding rise in reliance on prayer and miraculous healing (which are vastly popular in the United States today), including the use of chants, horoscopes, and amulets. Only a warped version of the classical culture of antiquity remained, and by 650, says Pierre Riché (see below), scholars in Gaul "were conscious of their role as the last defenders of the classical culture that distinguished them from the Barbarians." In Spain, Isidore of Seville tried to restore proper Latin pronunciation, but he was ridiculed by the clergy for his efforts. "Short of the mass destruction of the libraries," writes Radding, "a more complete collapse of a classical civilization is hard to imagine."

Levels of literacy were never high in the classical world, to be sure, yet William Harris, in *Ancient Literacy*, notes a rise in literacy among Roman citizens between 250 and 100 B.C., and a decline in the same during A.D. 200–400. A bourgeoisie had maintained a literate culture that was severely attenuated by the latter dates. We see a decline of urban elites, and of inscriptions on stone. The drop in literacy in the Roman Empire was particularly sharp after the third century. There was a decline in the availability of texts, for example, and the period saw a basic cultural shift, an extensive loss of awareness of past achievements in the writing of history, as well as in philosophy and literature. Even by A.D. 400, works by Cicero were difficult to find, and by the end of the sixth century, the very few leading intellectuals of the Latin West who did exist, such as Gregory of Tours (b. A.D. 538), could barely write coherent sentences. From Gregory's books, for example, we know that his spelling was faulty, his syntax shaky, and his arguments elementary. This is a far cry from the writings of Boethius, and it didn't take very long to happen. From A.D. 600 to 1000, most people forgot how to read or think, and, in fact, forgot that they had forgotten. There was an inability, says Radding, to approach texts critically, even among the "leading lights" of European culture, such as Alcuin of York in the eighth century. "Scholarship" consisted of collecting quotes and facts, and the reasoning used by these scholars in their own works bore little resemblance to the classical texts they admired. Real scholarly debates and understanding, genuine logical interaction, did not reappear until the eleventh century, when, for example, Berengar of Tours argued that the eucharistic wafer could not actually become the body of Christ. In fact, the mental landscape of the twelfth century was so different from that of the preceding six that it is only by this kind of bas-relief comparison that we see how dark the Dark Ages really were.

And so the proverbial lights went out in Western Europe. The parallels with contemporary America are not identical, to be sure, but they do seem a bit disturbing. Although our own disintegration, as stated earlier, will be unique, inasmuch as it is happening under the guise of "dynamic" transformation, it nevertheless contains similar elements. The factors of hype, ignorance, potential bankruptcy, and extreme social inequality are overwhelming, and they make a kind of spiritual death— apathy and classicist formalism—ultimately unavoidable. Hence, the real question to consider at this point is this: How, in the case of Rome, did the phoenix rise from the ashes six centuries later? After centuries of stagnation, what made the culture of the Latin West a viable option once more? And if them, why not us, and why not much more quickly? What are we going to have to do to preserve our culture during the coming dark age, and who is going to do it?

Before we can answer these questions, it might help to consider what the sources of cultural preservation were between roughly A.D. 500 and 1100, and what difference these made for the cultural reawakening of Western Europe that began toward the end of the eleventh century and then lurched unevenly toward the Italian Renaissance and the Scientific Revolution.

The traditional view—which is at least partly correct—is that during the sixth and seventh centuries, when the lights were going out, monasteries, especially Irish ones, began to stow away the nuggets of intellectual achievement from Roman civilization, and, to a lesser extent, that of Greece. By A.D. 700, writes the British historian Hugh Trevor-Roper, "European learning had fled to the bogs of Ireland." While Europe was sacked by Goths, Arabs, and Vikings, a few scholars such as the Venerable Bede (circa 673–735; lived at the Jarrow monastery in Northumbria) preserved a knowledge of the classics, carrying the seeds of Western life "through the grim winter of the Dark Ages." In the seventh century alone, two hundred new monasteries were founded in Gaul.

For three centuries, writes historian M. L. W. Laistner in *Thought and Letters in Western Europe*, Irish monasteries "produced a series of remarkable men who exerted a profound influence on thought and letters in Western Europe." Their missionary work extended to Scotland and the Continent, and disciples flocked to these regions. Monasteries such as those founded by the Irish monk Columba at Derry and Iona became important study centers, and in the early seventh century, Aidan, a monk at Iona, founded a new monastery and cultural center at Lindisfarne (an island off the coast of Northumberland). The seventh and eighth centuries were also a period of experimentation with the physical design of books and the technical processes of bookmaking, and the migration of English and Irish scholars to the Continent spread these techniques, which then had a profound influence on culture. Manuscripts and books proliferated due to successful scriptoria (copying rooms) and, later, cathedral libraries, many of which practiced a medieval form of interlibrary loan.

What went on in the monasteries? Well, the *lectio divina*, or divine reading, took up four hours of the daily routine and

functioned like a "great books" program. Supposedly, it gave
monks a literary culture. To this must be added the role of the
monastic school, the scriptorium, and the library. In theory at
least, the schools taught the old curriculum of the trivium
(grammar, rhetoric, and dialectic) and the quadrivium (arith-
metic, geometry, music, and astronomy), while the scriptorium
functioned as a kind of medieval publishing house, where the
classics were copied and illuminated manuscripts created,
which material then stocked the library. These formed the
most important book collections between the eighth and
twelfth centuries. Gradually, writes David Knowles in *Christian Monasticism*, the monasteries "became centres of light and
life in a simple, static, semi-barbarian world, preserving and
later diffusing what remained of ancient culture and spirituality." Or as the eminent historian Charles Homer Haskins said
of them: "Set like islands in a sea of ignorance and barbarism,
they had saved learning from extinction in Western Europe at
a time when no other forces moved toward that end."

The only trouble with this scenario is that history is never
this straightforward, and the role of the monasteries is no
exception. If monasticism preserved ancient learning, it often
did so in the process of trying to jettison it; and as even
Thomas Cahill admits (in *How the Irish Saved Civilization*),
the monks involved may have had no understanding of what
it was they were transcribing. There is an important object
lesson here, for this strange nonlinearity of history—its mad-
deningly dialectical quality—serves as a warning in terms of
any recommendations we might make for a renaissance in,
for example, the early twenty-second century. There are no
guarantees, and things can turn out other than originally
intended. With this in mind, let us look more closely at the
role of medieval monasticism in preserving the culture of the
Latin West.

One of the most comprehensive explorations of this issue is a rather thick volume by Pierre Riché entitled *Education and Culture in the Barbarian West*, which deals with the period from the collapse of the Roman Empire to the brief Carolingian renaissance of the eighth century. Three things stand out from Riché's careful study. One, there is no clear break between the end of one civilizational pattern and the beginning of another. It is not that Rome suddenly "collapsed" in 410 or 476 and medieval Europe suddenly "arose." What we have—again—is a *transformational* pattern—the persistence of fragments of the old civilization alongside the emergence of fragments of the new one. By 750, Europe was clearly medieval, but remnants of antiquity still hovered in the air. Second, this was a piecemeal process, which occurred without any discernible pattern. These fragments were typically unrelated, standing independently, without a clear sense as to why they were there. Brilliant flashes occured—a very few real, independent scholars such as John Scotus Erigena (ninth century), for example—but left no traces, vanishing as mysteriously as they had arisen. Finally, the monasticism that preserved the learning of classical antiquity was actually *opposed* to much of that tradition, and so preserved it in a religious form that ensured its survival, but at the expense of a good part of its content. As a result, its contribution to the renaissance of the twelfth century and beyond, although real, is nevertheless murky.

I have already alluded to this issue, at least in part, in my references to Charles Radding, who argues that by 600 even leading intellectuals were not able to think in the sense that the people of antiquity or of the twelfth century were able to do. Some sort of break in *mentalité* occurred, says Radding—the "substitution of imitative for conceptual intelligence." Thus Gregory I (Gregory the Great), one of the leading thinkers of

the sixth century, did not understand the notion of intentionality. For him, as for Isidore of Seville and virtually all intellectuals of the age (monks included), ideas were not ways of
viewing the world or analyzing a problem, but "objects" of a
sort. Such people, says Radding, probably did not understand
the implications of the texts they were copying. Passages got
transcribed without any inquiry as to whether they made
sense, or contradicted other authorities. In fact, many Benedictine monks had entered the monasteries as children, handed over by their parents. Scholarship consisted in the
compilation of quotes and facts, which were not used to support arguments but, rather, to render argumentation unnecessary. Thus the "reasoning" used by the scholars of the
Carolingian renaissance bore little resemblance to the reasoning employed by the classical authors they revered. So, for
example, monks made the writings of Boethius accessible, but
they never responded to what he was actually saying. Riché
agrees, asserting that although there was indeed a Carolingian
renaissance from 770 to 850, it was the continuation of a
patristic tradition (namely, that of the Church Fathers), not a
truly original episode.

Thus, it appears that the intellectual disciplines of distinction, definition, and dialectic were lost to the readers of the
Dark Ages. As may be happening today, this was more a "Jun-
gian" world than a world of cognitive understanding. The
apprehension of the world, in other words, rested on myth and
magic, and the prevalent mind-set was one of symbols, analo-
gies, and images. David Knowles guesses that much of what
the monks preserved was kept in cold storage rather than
transmitted, and Haskins notes that the focus of the Bene-
dictines was on chanting and Bible study. Haskins admits that
while the library and monastic school existed, real centers of
learning were very few. The seven liberal arts were largely inci-

dental. Intellectual life, in short, was actually quite humdrum.

Riché's argument, in any case, is not based on the notion of a shift in cognitive abilities, although what he argues does not really contradict the work of Charles Radding. His point is that monasteries, from the fourth century on, were not schools for sacred study but, rather, of ascetic practice, and this is largely what they remained. Christian scholarship—that is, theological study—had been vigorous down to the fifth century, but after that, it died out. Boethius had no disciples, and he lamented the ignorance of his contemporaries, while monks and clerics regarded philosophy as a source of heresy. By 500, the monastic ideal included the notion that learning was incompatible with Christian culture. The idea of the monastic school was to *break* with classical learning, and to teach the "science" of ascetic contemplation instead. We can thus point to the scriptoria as the loci of cultural preservation, but the copying of manuscripts was more of a manual training than an intellectual one: calligraphy rather than philosophy. The great monastery founded circa 410 on Saint Honorat (an island in the Lérins group, in the western Mediterranean) was specifically an ascetic center, and it became the model for many others. Saint Benedict, for example, founded Monte Cassino with the same idea in mind. It was intended that monks cut their ties to the world of antiquity, and the abbots led the way.

The goal, in other words, was "impregnation with the word of God," and even for educated men, the habit of personal reading was very difficult. Most of the reading, in any case, was of the Bible and the works of the Church Fathers, but, again, Riché doubts that the monks actually understood these texts. The *lectio* of the classical grammarians was, after all, about *interpretation*, a "Christian learning" in the sense that Augustine had understood it. The monastic *lectio* was something very different, part of an ascetic "healing." The goal was "purity of heart." Gregory of Tours' definition of the seven liberal arts, says Riché, "bears only slight resemblance to reality."

Thus the monastery founded at Vivarium, in Calabria, by Cassiodorus is often regarded as the great intellectual event of the second half of the sixth century, but the orientation was primarily ascetic, and the humanistic current that Cassiodorus cultivated did not survive his death. Nevertheless, when the library there was later dispersed, this literature did contribute to the renewal of studies in the West. The same can be said of Isidore of Seville, whose work touched only a very few, and bore fruit only much later as the result of the diffusion of his manuscripts.

The ascetic pattern can be seen everywhere. Lindisfarne may have been an important religious center, but it had no interest in classical education; nor was it intellectual study that Irish monks such as Columba were introducing into Gaul. Both he and Aidan (at Lindisfarne) renounced classical learning, implanting instead the desire to meditate on Scripture. Adomnán's *Life of St. Columba*, written nearly a century after Columba's death, consists almost entirely of miracle stories, even though its author, the ninth abbot of Iona, had devoted much of his life to scholarly and academic work. As far as we can determine, a good part of Columba's daily routine consisted of the reading of books and the copying of manuscripts, but the goal of this activity was religious and liturgical. Even Bede feared philosophy as leading to heresy, and he regarded secular literature as noxious. He did not explore the classics as literary works; rather, for him, as for other monks, there was no knowledge outside the circle of faith. The Anglo-Saxon clergy, says Riché, knew little or no Latin, and they were, in fact, as ignorant as the majority of laymen.

By 800, then, written civilization had disappeared, and only a tiny elite had access to intellectual culture. The Carolingians, says Riché, believed that they had rediscovered the works of ancient authors, but they were actually reading the *heirs* of these authors, as already indicated. And like the latter—writers such as Cassiodorus and Isidore—they were not interested in philosophy or real scholarship, but in appealing to the authority of the Church Fathers. It was only when schools multiplied, later on, and when antique works were recopied from accurate manuscripts, that genuine learning could occur.

And yet, this warped form of classical preservation did serve an important purpose. Manuscripts *were* copied, libraries *were* accumulated, and the later dispersion of this material made the subsequent revival of learning possible. Meditation on Scripture formed something of a basis for later intellectual investigation. When the "cognitive revolution" (Radding's "shift in *mentalité*") that began in the late eleventh century—itself part of a religious renewal—finally took hold, the ancient material was at least available, now to be looked at through new eyes. At that point, the recovery of texts coincided with the recovery of genuine intellectual habits.

So the texts had to be there for a twelfth-century renaissance to occur, and the monks of the Dark Ages managed to preserve them, even if they did not understand them very well and despite the fact that their own purposes were ascetic rather than intellectual. When, in 1115, the Benedictine abbot Guibert of Nogent produced an autobiography, he was able to recognize a fellow scholar and thinker in Augustine. But this is only half of the story of cultural renewal. What, exactly, was the cognitive shift of the twelfth century, and what were the factors that enabled it to occur?

The doyen of twelfth-century studies remains, even after seventy years, the historian Charles Homer Haskins, whose *Renaissance of the Twelfth Century* really defined the problem. Haskins emphasized the role of the classical tradition in the

intellectual reawakening of Europe, yet he assigned the largest
role to influences that came from outside the Latin West:
translators from the Greek and Arabic, for example. In his view,
the renaissance of the twelfth century was precipitated by
some sort of confluence of Latin Christian civilization with
other cultural traditions. Seventy years later, the picture has
shifted somewhat; most scholars of the period see the interest
in other cultures more as a *result* of the twelfth-century renaissance than as a cause of it. For texts—whether from classical
antiquity or from Moorish Spain—cannot by themselves pre-
cipitate anything. Both kinds of texts—"internal" as well as
"external"—had existed earlier without exercising this kind of
influence. Why was the twelfth century suddenly receptive to
them? Texts are a necessary condition for cultural renewal, but
not a sufficient one; and what Haskins omitted in his account
was the role of certain religious changes in making a new attitude toward learning possible. Haskins' account, in other
words, was that of a "secular renaissance." As I argue in *Coming to Our Senses*, the twelfth-century sense of religious renewal presupposed a new type of consciousness, which was part of
a growing sense of individualism, of an inner life and awareness of the self.

Following Charles Radding's remarks on the monastic
absence of intentionality in the early Middle Ages, we can
observe that the Church had no interest, in the case of sins, in
probing the conscience of the sinner. Penance simply consisted in behavioral reparation, or what was known as *satisfactio*,
and the sinner could even have a third party perform it, if he or
she wished. All that counted was that the penance be per-
formed. There was no interest in what would later (twelfth
century) be called *contritio*, interior repentance, in which the
sinner was made to search his soul and see the error of his
ways. The mind of the early Middle Ages, Church included,

did not think in these terms. In the same way, there are no references to direct spiritual experience, such as were witnessed and described by early figures such as Tertullian or Augustine. Faith was simply a matter of ritual and religious dogma. In the case of the law as well, there was virtually no discussion of the *intention* of the criminal, but only of the criminal act.

From about 1050 onward, all of this began to change. The law, for example, began to emphasize the relationship between intentionality and ethics, and, for the first time in many centuries, heresy suddenly emerged. Heretics began to deny the efficacy of ritual, arguing that things such as baptism required inward belief in order to work. "Waterless canals," they called the orthodoxy. Monastic communities began to awaken to the notion of interiority, or intense personal commitment. Romantic love, which had previously been very rare, now became something of a "movement" in the south of France; and mirrors, which had largely disappeared from use in the Dark Ages, became popular once again. By 1200, homicide with malice aforethought was singled out for special punishment—"Murder One," as American attorneys now call it.

This growing interest in introspection was thus institutional as well as individual. Guilt became a dominant theme, and the priest took on the role of confessor, or spiritual adviser. Saint Francis wrote that the monk should render service voluntarily, not, as Benedict had insisted in the sixth century, as a kind of mechanical reflex. Individual portraiture, which had been popular in antiquity and then absent thereafter, made a reappearance in the twelfth century. Even a phenomenon such as the Crusades would not have been possible without the "new" experience of inner awareness and personal religious commitment. The point is that interest in a real intellectual life—including an appreciation of the classics as well as of translations from the Greek and the Arabic—could not have arisen without the reemergence of a self to be interested in these things, and that process seems to have had a kind of spiritual or psychological shift at its center.

What was the cause of all this? Truth to tell, nobody knows. All we can point to is a series of social and economic changes that ran parallel to it, which may have been both cause and effect: the revival of urban centers, the rebirth of a middle class that had gone under in the fifth century, the existence of new sources of patronage and new intellectual centers. Nor do we know why these came into being. But in the early twelfth century, says the historian R. W. Southern, there were suddenly great numbers of individuals interested in new skills and knowledge for personal advancement and individual learning. These skills were now needed for high positions in Church government and administration, for example, and students began an aggressive search for competent teachers, as well as for new texts and new techniques of understanding. They needed these for the study of law, medicine, and nature, and they wanted to learn to argue and analyze. Similarly, John Baldwin writes that the twelfth-century renaissance was a revolution in education, as urban schools began to challenge the supremacy of monastic schools, and finally (after 1200) to grow into universities. Other historians have pointed to the rising world of laissez-faire, of rapid economic growth in craft, trade, and business. From 1100 on, there was an expansion of family-owned private property, and a concomitant need for lay professionals, such as secular scribes, notaries, and lawyers. This necessitated a revival of Latin studies, since things such as charters, court decisions, and records were written in Latin. In an essay entitled "Classicism and Style in Latin Literature," Janet Martin argues that the vitality of the twelfth century is revealed in the quality and abundance of Latin literature.

Manuals on writing and composition began to appear around 1070, and there was a conscious adaptation of the styles of Seneca, Sallust, Cicero, and Quintilian, all at a very high level. Latin poetry also flowered during this time, with a corresponding sensitivity to grammatical correctness and the range of effects possible in verse.

If this were a New Age book, or a Hollywood movie, my task would be a lot simpler. I could just say, Look, Rome fell, but then all of these monks (led, in the film version, by Arnold Schwarzenegger) ran around preserving culture, and that led to a renaissance later on; so what we need to do is form a new monastic class to do the same thing today, and America will be saved. There is—possibly—a potential grain of truth to this, but the case study of the present chapter makes it clear that history follows no such simple cause-and-effect pattern. The greater wisdom is that of Karl Marx: "Men make their own history," he wrote, "but they do not make it just as they please. . . . " They each have individual intentions, he says, but the final outcome is something that no particular person expected or planned.

The lessons derived from Rome and medieval Europe are not straightforward ones, and if the phenomenon of the monastic option does repeat itself in the twenty-first century, we can be sure that it will not do so in exactly the same way as before, which is good. After all, if the medieval monks had ascetic purposes, and preserved texts that they frequently did not understand, then this would be a peculiar model for a monastic class of today to emulate. One might even argue that the process of preserving classical learning by accident, as it were, only served to *retard* the coming of the twelfth-century renaissance. Nor do I think that institutionalization would be the best vehicle for cultural transmission today, because finally we are talking about individual habits of mind that cannot and should not be channeled by means of "structures." If this is going to work, it must be spontaneous and natural, part of the air we eventually come to breathe. Institutions have a clever way of killing all that. When I say, then, that I am optimistic about contemporary "monastic" possibilities, it represents no more than an educated guess on my part, and maybe it is just wishful thinking; history remains a strange and unpredictable creature. But this much I do know: If we make *no* attempt to preserve the best in our culture, we can rest assured that the possibility of cultural renewal is pretty much ruled out. Convolutions of the Middle Ages notwithstanding, the availability of the Greco-Roman heritage, in whatever form, was a necessary, if not sufficient, condition for subsequent cultural revival.

In terms of a future renewal, much of it will depend on a commitment to individualism, something that has been much maligned in recent years. We hear so much trendy, tedious talk today of how bad individualism is, and how we need to think in terms of "the group." The problem is that the group usually offers conformity, not genuine community. The drift in the United States today is toward the submergence of the self into the Mass Mind, a trend that is powerfully encouraged by corporate culture and the new technology. Along with this—as in the early Middle Ages—we see the dissolution of interiority, and the loss or denigration of individual judgment and achievement. All this is a major factor in the disintegration of American culture, which, popular opinion to the contrary, is a herd culture, not an individualistic one. Thus political scientist Kenneth Minogue writes that the fashionable attack on individualism amounts to "a project for closing down the innovative vitality of the modern world." An important aspect of the new monastic option is thus a rejection of this project, of the group, and of attempts at institutionalization. Today's "monk" is committed to a *renewed* sense of self, and to the avoidance of groupthink, including anticorporate or anti–consumer culture groupthink. The monastic option will not be served by the new monastic "class" being a class of any sort. As the quote from E. M. Forster on page 9 shows, the power of this contribution lies precisely in its *lack* of institutionalization. Membership cards and badges (whether real or metaphorical), avant-garde language and appropriate party line, organization and even visibility—these are the exact opposite of what the monastic option is about. We don't need to form our own little institutes or committees; that would be the kiss of death. In *The Dark Side of the Left*, Richard Ellis shows how avant-garde political movements, including environmentalism and feminism, become utopian, Manichaean, and finally tyrannical; but he admits that this is a right-wing tendency as well. The point is, it is a *group* tendency. The more individual the activity is, and the more out of the public eye, the more effective it is likely to be in the long run. Not that like-minded souls shouldn't make connections, but the key is to keep these links informal. As Kenneth Minogue rightly notes, Western individualists have a capacity for joint action that exceeds that of communally organized civilizations.

Finally, as already indicated, we possess a major advantage over the original medieval form of the monastic option, one that I suspect could considerably speed up the process of cultural renewal: We *know* what we are preserving, and why. Unlike the monks of the early Middle Ages, we are not reading texts we cannot understand, or arguing for ways of thinking or living that are the opposite of the intended outcome. While this does not mean that our actions will have a direct effect— or, indeed, *any* effect, for all we know—it does lend a clarity of purpose to this activity that can only be beneficial. I shall say more about this in Chapter 4. For now, I wish to offer a brief digression, and say a few words about the monastic option in literature. Although this is not very extensive, a few authors in the science fiction genre, of all places, have recognized the pattern I am referring to and have tried to draw out its implications for today. A brief "intermezzo" on the subject, then, might not be out of place.

THE TESTIMONY
OF LITERATURE

. . . our fears of a new "dark age" in which civilization
itself, as we have known it, may disappear or be
confined to small islands of archaic conservation . . .
—George Steiner,
In Bluebeard's Castle

The potential "career" of the monastic option in postmodern
times is the subject of Walter Miller's brilliant futuristic novel,
A Canticle for Leibowitz, which has become a classic of the sci-
fi genre. The story begins in the twenty-sixth century A.D., with
Brother Francis, a monk in the Order of Saint Leibowitz (soon
to be canonized), keeping a Lenten vigil in the Utah desert.
Poking through some ruins, Francis stumbles on an underground fallout shelter dating from the middle of the twentieth
century—"the twilight period of the Age of Enlightenment."
There he finds a rusty metal box with some papers in it, which,
amazingly enough, belonged to Leibowitz himself. Francis has
uncovered the relics of the saint.

The historical background to this is that of nuclear war,
which occurred in the second half of the twentieth century.
The horror of this event led the remaining population to rise up
against the few scientists and scholars still around. The mob,

which proudly took the name "Simpletons," eventually mar-
tyred anyone who was literate at all. Isaac Edward Leibowitz,
apparently, had been some sort of technician, or perhaps electrical engineer, and (legend had it) fled to a Cistercian
monastery for shelter. There he became a priest, and later
founded a new community dedicated to the protection of culture from the Simpletons, and to the preservation of it for
future generations. Monks in this order were either "bookleg-
gers," who smuggled books into the southwestern desert and
buried them, or "memorizers," who memorized entire volumes
of history, literature, and science. From the vast storehouse of
knowledge that existed in the twentieth century, only a few
kegs of books were saved, however, and Leibowitz himself was
murdered by the mob during the course of a booklegging mission. For the next six centuries, in any case, monks copied the
Memorabilia, for a time when humanity would once again prefer light to darkness.

The problem with all of this scribal activity, however, was—
as in the case of the European Dark Ages—that the copyists
did not really know what they were actually copying. The
papers discovered by Brother Francis, for example, contain a
grocery list Leibowitz had scribbled (reminding him to buy
pastrami, bagels, and sauerkraut), along with a circuit-design
blueprint labeled "Transistorized Control System for Unit Six-
B." Francis spends the next fifteen years producing an illuminated copy of the latter on vellum, complete with elaborate
scrollwork and gold inlay. In a similar way, twentieth-century
algebra texts are copied and embellished with olive leaves,
and with "cheerful cherubim surrounding tables of loga-
rithms." "Without your work," the Pope later tells Brother Francis, "the world's amnesia might well be total."

That transistor diagrams and delicatessen shopping lists

become sacred texts is a fine bit of satire, of course, but it may not be so far off the mark. Miller anticipates not only Charles Radding but also those scholars who maintain that classical culture was preserved unwittingly. This knowledge, writes Miller, was empty of content, and yet

> such knowledge had a symbolic structure that was peculiar to itself, and at least the symbol-interplay could be observed. To observe the way a knowledge-system is knit together is to learn at least a minimum knowledge-of-knowledge, until someday—someday, or some century—an Integrator would come, and things would be fitted together again. So time mattered not at all. The Memorabilia was there, and it was given to them to preserve, and preserve it they would if the darkness in the world lasted ten more centuries, or even ten thousand years. . . .

As it turns out, the wait (from the twentieth century) takes about twelve hundred years. The scene shifts to the thirty-second century; a new renaissance is afoot. The present abbot of the Order of Leibowitz, Dom Paulo, reflects on this in a passage that is central to the dialectical nature of the monastic option:

> For twelve centuries, a small flame of knowledge had been kept smoldering in the monasteries; only now were their minds ready to be kindled. Long ago, during the last age of reason, certain proud thinkers had claimed that valid knowledge was indestructible—that ideas were deathless and truth immortal. But that was true only in the subtlest sense, the abbot thought, and not superficially true at all. There was objective meaning in the world, to be sure: the nonmoral *logos* or design of the Creator; but such meanings were God's

and not Man's, until they found an imperfect incarnation, a
dark reflection, within the mind and speech and culture of
a given human society, which might ascribe values to the
meanings so that they became valid in a human sense within the culture. For Man was a culture-bearer as well as a
soul-bearer, but his cultures were not immortal and they
could die with a race or an age, and then human reflections
of meaning and human portrayals of truth receded, and truth
and meaning resided, unseen, only in the objective *logos* of
Nature and the ineffable *Logos* of God. Truth could be cru-
cified; but soon, perhaps, a resurrection.

Miller continues:

The Memorabilia was full of ancient words, ancient for-
mulae, ancient reflections of meaning, detached from minds
that had died long ago, when a different sort of society had
passed into oblivion. There was little of it that could still be
understood. Certain papers seemed as meaningless as a Bre-
viary would seem to a shaman of the nomad tribes. Others
retained a certain ornamental beauty or an orderliness that
hinted of meaning, as a rosary might suggest a necklace to a
nomad. The earliest brothers of the Leibowitzian Order had
tried to press a sort of Veronica's Veil to the face of a cruci-
fied civilization; it had come away marked with an image of
the face of ancient grandeur, but the image was faintly printed, incomplete, and hard to understand. The monks had
preserved the image, and now it still survived for the world
to inspect and try to intepret if the world wanted to do so.
The Memorabilia could not, of itself, generate a revival of
ancient science or high civilization, however, for cultures
were begotten by the tribes of Man, not by musty tomes; but
the books could help, Dom Paulo hoped—the books could
point out directions and offer hints to a newly evolving science. It had happened once before. . . .

THE TWILIGHT OF AMERICAN CULTURE   95

Research into the Leibowitzian documents by one of the new scientists—a kind of Leonardo figure—leads to an appreciation of what the science and culture of the twentieth century were all about. Many of his discoveries, he comes to see, are really *re*discoveries. How minds arose that, for the first time in twelve hundred years, could appreciate this material is not made clear by Miller (any more than it is by Charles Homer Haskins et al.); but the new generation absorbs everything it can from the Memorabilia and then moves on. In the final section of the book, which takes place in the thirty-eighth century, we see the result, a new techno-secular civilization.

Unfortunately, the old pattern recurs. The brilliance of this resurrected civilization brings about its own demise. Nuclear war occurs once again, and some members of the Order of Lei-bowitz flee in a spaceship to stellar colonies, taking the Memorabilia with them. The spaceship becomes their monastery, outer space their new desert or wilderness. They will eventually send missions to other space colonies, where monks in copy centers will once again copy material they do not understand and preserve it for the next cycle of Enlightenment. For Miller, the historical process is perforce recurrent; there is no alternative to this endless "boom and bust cycle" of the mind:

> Listen, are we helpless? Are we doomed to do it again and again and again? Have we no choice but to play the Phoenix in an unending sequence of rise and fall? Assyria, Babylon, Egypt, Greece, Carthage, Rome, the Empires of Charle-magne and the Turk. Ground to dust and plowed with salt. Spain, France, Britain, America—burned into the oblivion of the centuries. And again and again and again.
> *Are we doomed to it, Lord, chained to the pendulum of our own mad clockwork, helpless to halt its swing?*

All-out nuclear war, of course, is just a literary device here;
it is not a prerequisite for contemporary cultural disintegration,
and indeed, one could argue that corporate consumer culture
is tantamount to a kind of nuclear attack on the mind. The
issue is thus deeper than this device, and, I believe, even deeper than Tainter's theory of declining marginal returns or Spengler's notion of the death of the soul. Miller is positing a
dialectical relationship between knowledge and faith, almost
along the lines of original sin: Increase of secular knowledge,
mastery, and control finally results in hubris, loss of meaning,
and self-destruction; whereupon, a Dark Age of faith ensues,
paradoxically bearing within itself the seeds of secular intelligence that a monastic class will cultivate later on, wittingly
or not.

A second example of the monastic option in literature is
Ray Bradbury's novel *Fahrenheit 451*. I have made previous
reference to the movie version of this work, but it will be helpful to say something about the text itself, which, appearing in
its earliest version in 1950, is extraordinarily prescient. Leaving aside the issue of direct censorship of books—rendered
unnecessary by McWorld, as it turns out, since most people
don't read anymore—most of the features of this futuristic
society are virtually upon us, or perhaps no more than twenty
years away.

As already indicated, the society depicted in *Fahrenheit 451*
has banned books and immerses itself intead in video entertainment, a kind of "electronic Zen," in which history has been
forgotten and only the present moment counts. The central
character, Guy Montag, is a "fireman"—that is, his job is to
locate renegades who have sequestered books, arrest the former, and burn the latter. He has done this for ten years, living
a banal but undisturbed existence, when he begins talking to
Clarisse, the sixteen-year-old girl who lives next door. She has

been labeled "antisocial," but as she puts it, "It all depends on what you mean by social, doesn't it?" High school classes, she tells Montag, are devoid of any real content, and the whole thing is dangerous anyway. "They kill each other," she says; "six of my friends have been shot in the last year alone." When Clarisse hangs out in subways or at soda fountains, and eavesdrops on conversations, she discovers that people don't really talk about anything: "They name a lot of cars or clothes or swimming pools mostly and nobody says anything different from anyone else." Her uncle, she says, told her that in his grandfather's time, students had responsibilities, no one got murdered in the schools, and people had things of value to say. In any case, she admits, she hasn't any real friends, and is labeled "abnormal"; but there's no one to be friends with anyway, so what's the difference?

Partly through contact with Clarisse, Montag begins reading some of the books he confiscates, aware that, in the language of Walter Miller, he is surrounded by Simpletons. He falls ill and cannot go in to work. Finally, his boss, Beatty, who curiously enough knows something about cultural history, pays him a visit and takes it upon himself to explain to Montag how their profession came to be. "The fact is," he tells Montag,

> we didn't get along well until photography came into its own. Then—motion pictures in the early twentieth century. Radio. Television. Things began to have mass. . . . And because they had mass, they became simpler. . . . Films and radios, magazines, books leveled down to a sort of pastepudding norm. . . .

Everything was designed for a quick sell, everything had to have a snap ending, until finally the cultural pattern became: "Out of the nursery into the college and back to the nursery."

Life turned into slogans, sound bites; the goal was to whirl the mind around "under the pumping hands of publishers, exploiters, [and] broadcasters. . . ." He goes on:

> School is shortened, discipline relaxed, philosophies, histories, languages dropped. English and spelling gradually neglected, finally almost completely ignored. . . . Why learn anything save pressing buttons, pulling switches, fitting nuts and bolts?

Magazines "became a nice blend of vanilla tapioca," and books were turned into "dishwater." As a result, censorship wasn't even necessary, because practically no one was buying books anyway. Technology and mass exploitation had carried the day. *Intellectual* became a dirty word. Finally, censorship and burning of books were instituted as an afterthought, a kind of icing on the cake, to ensure that the leveling process was complete; that no one was different from anybody else, so that all could finally be "happy."

Montag later expresses his angst to Faber, an English professor who had been dismissed forty years before, when the last liberal arts college was forced to shut down because of lack of students and financial support. (For some odd reason, Faber's college didn't hit on the idea of turning its curricula into tapioca or dishwater.) Faber tells him that, yes, they might form underground classes in thinking and reading, but "that would just nibble the edges." The cancer is far too advanced for these sorts of trifles: "Our civilization is flinging itself to pieces. Stand back from the centrifuge." Faber also confirms Beatty's analysis, adding that the fireman's job is really superfluous now, a circus act of sorts, because "the public itself stopped reading of its own accord." "I remember the newspapers dying like huge moths," he says; "no one *wanted* them back. No one missed them."

Montag finally escapes to the outskirts of the city, where he locates people who hide in the woods, memorize the classics, and then teach them to their children. This is, of course, the heart of the monastic option, and Bradbury sums it up as follows:

> Someday, some year, [when] the books can be written again, the [forest] people will be called in, one by one, to recite what they know and we'll set it in type until another Dark Age, when we might have to do the whole damn thing over again. But that's the wonderful thing about man: he never gets so discouraged or disgusted that he gives up doing it all over again, because he knows very well it is important and *worth* the doing.

For Bradbury, too, then, the process is cyclical; civilizations rise and fall, and a class of "monks" is always necessary to preserve the treasures of the dying civilization and use them, like seeds, to impregnate a new one. In the process, they create an authentic life for themselves; the personal benefits of such activity are as important as the possible historical outcome.

My final example focuses more on the issue of power as it affects these cycles, rather than on cultural preservation as such, though the latter is certainly present, once again, in the form of buried knowledge. In *This Perfect Day* (1970), Ira Levin depicts a society about three hundred years into the future, not unlike Huxley's *Brave New World*, in which social engineering has been taken to its logical end point. There are no problems in this society because, in a fundamental sense, there are no people. By this time, there has been enough genetic alteration and psychiatric reprogramming (brought on by drugs) to turn the mass of people into contented robots. A tiny technological elite, at the control center known as UNI, has managed to create a stable, "perfect" life for all, a utopia that is also a nightmare (from our point of view). As in *Fahrenheit 451*, we have a mass society that has lost all genuine diversity and individualism. It is, in a sense, a large mental hospital, with everyone required to take a daily dose of tranquilizers and wear bracelet IDs that monitor their every move. This ensures that any creative or independent thinking stays deeply repressed, and that the political power remains in the hands of UNI's technological elite. It all looks like a corporate theme park, in effect, and it is clear that Levin saw our society, in 1970, as heading in that direction (a less shocking prediction thirty years later, I would think). The hero of the novel, Chip, for a host of complicated reasons, becomes disillusioned with the UNI world and learns how to deceive the controllers and reduce his daily drug intake. As his head begins to clear, he meets a few other individuals who have stumbled onto the possibility of freedom and detoxification, and who have also begun to lead double lives. They break into the "pre-UNI museum," which records, in effect, the lost world of the Enlightenment tradition, in which creativity, art, and individual choice were the order of the day. Chip and his friends sort through the ancient texts in the museum and piece together a picture of what pre-UNI life must have been like. After a number of elaborate twists and turns, Chip decides that the only solution to the cultural hypnosis and political control exerted by UNI is to take it on and destroy it. In an Ian Fleming–like way, he undertakes the cosmic battle required, coming face-to-face in the process with evil incarnate, the rulers of UNI, a man named Wei (over two hundred years old) and his select group of disciples.

It turns out that a cycle of rebellion and cooptation has been in place for a very long time. That is, the ruling circle assumes that anyone clever enough to slip through the fine mesh of their surveillance, locate the truth about the past, and assault the control center must be extremely smart—one of them, in fact. Hence, Wei offers Chip power, an entrée into the club. "There's *joy* in having it," he tells Chip; "in controlling, in being the only one. That's the absolute truth. . . ." Part of Chip was always tempted by this lure, but his assault is finally not on UNI, but on power itself. Even if the "enlightened" run UNI, he realizes, it's still UNI. If his strategy had been one of replacement, he sees, he would eventually have turned into Wei. What's the point? Ultimately, there is no replacement strategy. So the story ends on a curious note—curious from the viewpoint of civilization, at least.

There is, nonetheless, a lost world of knowledge that is recovered; as I said, that of the Enlightenment tradition. The point Levin is trying to make via this monk/rebel drama is that the life of "harmonic convergence" is no life at all; that our real sources of vitality lie in a tradition—perhaps best represented by Voltaire—of healthy skepticism, individual creativity, and free choice. This, and not a life organized around power, is *real* intelligence, which is why he has Chip walk away from the opportunity to become the new Wei. "Knowing the truth," writes Levin, "would be a different kind of happiness—a more satisfactory kind, I think, even if it turned out to be a sad kind." I doubt Voltaire could have said it better. The point is that only this kind of honesty can break the cycle of "replacement strategy," but, as in *This Perfect Day*, it is unclear where this leaves us. I shall return to the problem of power at the conclusion of this book.

It is also unclear whether civilizations, or, more generally, world systems, necessarily obey a logic of expansion and decline; why a cyclical movement of expansion/contraction has to exist at all. Miller, as we have seen, was obsessed with this

question, which might be put as follows: Do societies possess
some sort of mechanism whereby, in the process of expansion,
they discover a great truth and then push it to the point that
it doubles back and then turns on that society in the form of
a lie? If such is the case, this mechanism might tell us a
lot about the dynamics of collapse and restructuring in the
twenty-first century.

THE DIALECTIC OF ENLIGHTENMENT

Such was all the nod needed to turn a handful of harmless beans into a beanstalk that, in time, outgrew the world's terrarium. The limited-liability corporation: the last noble experiment, loosing an unknowable outcome upon its beneficiaries. Its success outstripped all rational prediction until, gross for gross, it became mankind's sole remaining endeavor.

—Richard Powers,
Gain

Under existing conditions, the gifts of fortune themselves become elements of misfortune. . . . Progress becomes regression.

—Max Horkheimer and Theodor Adorno,
The Dialectic of Enlightenment

There's a lot to be said for civilization as it was before the Enlightenment got vertigo. . . .

—Ronald Wright,
A Scientific Romance

The question of why Western civilization seems to be governed by recurrent oscillations was the particular research focus of the eminent sociologist Pitirim Sorokin, who presented his findings in a four-volume work published during the period 1937–1941. *Social and Cultural Dynamics* is a work that, like those of Miller and Bradbury, is eerily prescient about our present situation, especially given the fact that it was written in the late 1930s. Sorokin argues that civilization in general falls into two fundamental categories, which he labels "ideational" and "sensate." Ideational cultures, he claims, are spiritual or ascetic in nature, and they focus primarily on the transformation of man's inner life, whereas sensate cultures, such as our own, are materialistic, based on the modification of the external world. The former are theological, the latter rational or scientific. Sorokin also identifies an intermediate position between these two which he calls "idealistic," which involves a harmonious synthesis of faith, reason, and empiricism. This configuration, in his view, is rare, having been dominant in the West only during the fifth and fourth centuries B.C. in Greece, and in Western Europe from roughly A.D. 1200 to 1350.

The classic ideational period, says Sorokin, occurred between 500 and 1100, when faith was dominant within a Christian matrix. "If at any period in the history of the Western mentality the philosophers and the people as a whole felt that they were in possession of the truth," he writes, "it was in these centuries. There was no skepticism, no questioning, no doubt, no relativity, no hesitation, no reservation." The truth was monolithic and theocentric. We see very few scientific discoveries between the seventh and eleventh centuries, as the dominant mentality shifted to the suprasensory world and truth was couched in symbolic language. When empiricism finally did reappear in the late eleventh century, a period of organic unity ensued. As in the earlier Greek period, knowledge was not narrowed to one vista or reduced to one source. Thomas Aquinas, says Sorokin, was the high point of this late medieval period, creating a blend of sensory, intellectual, and divine knowledge. But this delicate balance could not hold. Empiricism gained too much ground, and with the Renaissance and its aftermath we entered a period that proved to be the reverse of the previous monolithic theocentrism. By the early twentieth century, this culture began to show signs of fatigue and self-destruction, and Sorokin suggests that a new ideational phase is in the process of being born.

This pendulum swing between religious and scientific extremes constitutes, in Sorokin's view, a "dialectical destiny." The supposedly balanced periods of harmonious integration, which are few and fleeting, occur only when an age of faith breaks up, such as happened in the case of the twelfth century renaissance. They do not occur when a sensate age collapses, when you just get a return to faith. The pattern, he says, suggests that an age of faith is now dawning, will become dominant and excessive, but then will run *its* course and eventually give way to a sensate age once again.

This is not very different from the view of Walter Miller, except that Miller could not explain why such a phenomenon occurred. For Sorokin, however, the mechanism of this dialectical destiny is an internal one. This, he believes, is because each of these positions contains only a part of the truth, and in their extreme forms—which is what we inevitably get—they involve more untruth than truth. This explains why the pendulum swings back and forth. Cultures dominated by one-sided mentalities fall victim to their own parochialism. The untruth evokes a strong reaction, which eventually evokes an opposite strong reaction, and so on. Philosophically, this analysis has much in common with the dialectics of Aristotle or Hegel, in which any reality is seen to contain the seeds of its own negation. Hence, over time, it produces its antithesis. History thus keeps repeating itself, although never in an identical form. Instead, we get an incessant variation on recurrent themes.

The uncanny aspect of Sorokin's analysis is that his predictions for the twenty-first century are already showing up. Sorokin foretells that the boundary between true and false will erode, and that conscience (superego) will disappear in favor of special-interest groups. Force and fraud will become the norm, he says; the family will disintegrate; real creativity will wane. As a substitute for the latter, we shall get a multitude of mediocre pseudothinkers, and our belief system will turn into a strange, inchoate stew of shreds of science, philosophy, and magic. Above all—anticipating here the rise of kitsch—"quantitative colossalism will substitute for qualitative refinement." Instead of classics, we shall have best-sellers; instead of genius, technique. Real thought will be supplanted by information. Security will fade, and catastrophe will ensue. Culture will become increasingly debased, emptied of content, until a reaction or catharsis will finally take place, after which a new ideational culture will arise from the ashes of the old sensate one.

Although heuristically valuable, Sorokin's outline contains a number of dubious features. For one, he regards the shift to ideational culture as a positive thing, despite the fact that the last incarnation of it was that of the European Dark Ages and despite his admission that this was an unrelenting age of dogma. Second, Sorokin's assessment of the "turn," the point at which sensate culture "went bad," as it were, is purely subjective, and much too early in any case—A.D. 1350. To be sure, much was lost with the rise of a scientific civilization; but to call the Renaissance and the Scientific Revolution a "decline" is possible only for those who share a severe antimodernist bias (Michel Foucault, for example). The period from 1350 to 1850 was surely Europe's most fertile and creative era. But Sorokin would seem to be right in terms of an operative dialectical dynamic. What starts out as liberating becomes, in the fullness of time, precisely that which is suffocating. We need to pursue this notion of a dialectical destiny, then, but in a more credible way.

The matter of "what went wrong" has intrigued a number of great twentieth-century thinkers and critics of technology, such as Martin Heidegger and Jacques Ellul, but it probably received its most detailed expression in the work of the Frankfurt School for Social Research—that of Max Horkheimer and Theodor Adorno in particular, and its American representative, Herbert Marcuse. In *The Dialectic of Enlightenment*, Horkheimer and Adorno identified the problem quite clearly, arguing that Enlightenment thought slowly got transmuted into scientism and positivism. In this scheme of things, everything got objectified; only that which was measurable and empirical was regarded as real. The logical endpoint of this is a purely technocratic *Weltanschauung*, the vision of a totally administered world. The original freshness and strength of Enlightenment thought was its critical element; but as it became a tool of the existing social and political order, it started to convert the positive values it was elected to defend into "something negative and destructive." So if political freedom is inseparable from Enlightenment thought, that thought nevertheless contained the seeds of a reversal. For modernity eventually issued out into the commercial society, which became a metaphysics in its own right. "The consumer," concluded Horkheimer and Adorno, "becomes the ideology of the pleasure industry, whose institutions he cannot escape." And in fact, utilitarianism is the real, and pervasive (if invisible) philosophy of American society, a society in which very little has value in and of itself.

As a characterization of the twentieth century, and perhaps even much of the nineteenth, the views of the Frankfurt

School have much to recommend them. The problem is that it extended its analysis to the Scientific Revolution, and occasionally even back to the rationalism of the ancient Greeks. Thus in *One-Dimensional Man*, Herbert Marcuse indicts the thought of the seventeenth century as being inherently "purposive-rational," inherently antithetical to any values except those embedded in science and technology, which he says wear the mask of neutrality. Science, says Marcuse, is purely about the abstract and rational manipulation of the environment; it reduces everything to instrumental value, in the guise of being value-free.

There is, of course, some truth in this, that the seeds of the modern dilemma are buried in a methodology that is four hundred years old. But seeds are not trees, and in that sense, if I may mix metaphors, there is a tendency here to throw the baby out with the bathwater. For what this analysis ignores is the context in which thinkers such as William Harvey or Galileo were operating. By the late sixteenth century, Church Aristotelianism and medieval science were, as one scholar put it, little more than "petrified drivel." Medicine was still dominated by the thought of Galen (second century A.D.); geocentricity was looking increasingly quaint. The whole framework of argument by syllogism and deductive reasoning had become hopelessly stultifying, and thus the discovery not merely of new facts but of a whole new methodology was, to the thinkers of the seventeenth century, akin to suddenly breathing pure oxygen after centuries of living underwater. It was immensely liberating, and ultimately tore down political notions of divine right and organic hierarchy. Indeed, the French and American revolutions would have been impossible without the new scientific worldview, of which Voltaire and Thomas Jefferson were the logical heirs.

This is not the place to review the history of the Scientific Revolution; quite obviously, many historians have already done so, and in exhaustive detail. But let me provide a few quotations from one particular source, the *Novum Organum* (1620) of Francis Bacon, just to give the reader some idea of the "fresh air" aspect of this revolution in thought, the sense of breaking free from the dead hand of the past and at long last being able to breathe. Bacon wrote:

Again there is another great and powerful cause why the sciences have made but little progress [up to now]; which is this. It is not possible to run a course aright when the goal itself has not been rightly placed. Now the true and lawful goal of the sciences is none other than this: that human life be endowed with new discoveries and powers. (Aphorism 81)

For rightly is truth called the daughter of time, not of authority. (Aphorism 84)

There is no hope except in a new birth of science; that is, in raising it regularly up from experience and building it afresh; which no one (I think) will say has yet been done or thought of. (Aphorism 97)

My purpose . . . is to try whether I cannot in very fact lay more firmly the foundations, and extend more widely the limits, of the power and greatness of man. (Aphorism 116)

For I am building in the human understanding a true model of the world, such as it is in fact, not such as a man's own reason would have it to be; a thing which cannot be done without a very diligent dissection and anatomy of the world. (Aphorism 124)

And finally, this ringing manifesto from *The Parasceve*:

For the [natural] history that I require and design, special
care is to be taken that it be of wide range and made to the
measure of the universe. For the world is not to be narrowed
till it will go into the understanding (which has been done
hitherto), but the understanding is to be expanded and
opened till it can take in the image of the world.

There is something glorious about these declarations, ones
that build on the momentum of humanism that can be seen
in the notebooks of Leonardo da Vinci or in the writings of
Pico della Mirandola (*Oration on the Dignity of Man*). We can
do it, Bacon is saying; we can free ourselves from the shack-
les of Aristotelianism and the Middle Ages and come into our
own. "For new discoveries must be sought from the light of
nature," he tells his readers, "not fetched back out of the
darkness of antiquity." And with that affirmation came the triumph of the rational-empirical method, that truth depends
on evidence, experiment, and analysis. You have to *prove* what
you say, rather than appeal to religion or authority, and this
became the touchstone of the Enlightenment ("Dare to
think!" cried Immanuel Kant) and of modernity in general. It
lies at the heart of parliamentary democracy, the Western
judicial system, and of our understanding of biological evolution and the physical world. Give that up, and we are, in
fact, finished.

What, then, went wrong? The problem is not with the scientific method per se, without which no healthy democracy
can function, but with its integration into, and evolution within, the context of an expanding industrial, technological, and
now global corporate/commercial culture. Did science make
that culture possible? Of course; it was a necessary, though
hardly sufficient, condition. Is it *equivalent* to that culture?
Not at all.

The story is something like this: For all of the eighteenth century, and most of the nineteenth, technology did more for science than science did for technology. It was the Industrial Revolution, in other words, that put the Scientific Revolution on the map, that—starting with England—wove science into the nation's life. There is a large body of literature on this, but perhaps the most famous example is the formulation of the laws of thermodynamics. By 1840, the steam engine was the basis of the new industrial economy in Great Britain. Energy had become a marketable quantity, and there was a need to find a measurable mechanical equivalent of this energy: How much work can you get per unit of fuel burned? Engineers such as James Prescott Joule began to evaluate engines in terms of their capacity to raise weights, and this led Joule (along with several others, such as Sadi Carnot in France) to formulate the first law of thermodynamics, or what is known as the law of the conservation of energy. It was, in short, practice that benefited theory, rather than the reverse.

In general, the technological innovations of this period of industrial take-off were the product of unlettered "tinkerers." John Kay, weaver and mechanic, invented the flying shuttle in 1733; James Hargreaves, weaver and carpenter, invented the spinning jenny about 1765; Richard Arkwright, a barber, was responsible for the water frame, patented in 1770; and the "mule," a combination of the jenny and the water frame, was the result of the efforts of Samuel Crompton, a mechanic. Edmund Cartwright, the man responsible for the power loom, in 1785, studied literature at Oxford, but he had no scientific education, and he hired a carpenter and blacksmith to help him in his work. In the case of the famous "puddling" process, by which pig iron is converted into malleable form, this was independently discovered by Peter Onions, a foreman in an iron mill, and Henry Cort, a navy contractor. Neither of these men had any knowledge of chemistry, and it is unlikely that the chemistry of the eighteenth century could have helped them in any event. What they did was to put compounds that happened to be rich in iron oxides into a furnace to take the carbon out of the pig iron by forming carbon dioxide; but this was purely trial and error. Oxygen had been discovered only a few years before this, and they were hardly aware that carbon dioxide was being released. The names of Priestley and Lavoisier were unknown to them, and it was only in the next century that chemistry, after the fact, could *explain* how puddling worked. In all of these cases, science contributed nothing to technology and industrialization in the early stages of the Industrial Revolution. The chemistry of fertilizers, for example, was born only in the 1840s, through the work of Justus von Liebig.

There is, however, one possible exception, and it is notable because it *is* an exception: the invention of the separate condenser by James Watt. To obtain coal, copper, and tin from mines, something was needed to drive pumps in order to drain the mines. The first atmospheric engine that could convert heat to work was invented by a blacksmith named Thomas Newcomen in the early eighteenth century. It was, however, grossly inefficient, because the main cylinder that formed a vacuum and thereby drove the pump had to be alternately rendered hot and cold, at a great waste of fuel. Watt's contribution was to devise a separate cylinder for condensation so that the main cylinder could be kept hot at all times. Yet this was not quite a process of trial and error. Watt was a maker of scientific instruments, and he drew up pressure-volume diagrams in order to estimate how much steam a given amount of water could condense. He discovered that converting steam to water at 212° F yielded an unexpectedly large amount of heat, and he took these results to the chemist Joseph Black at the University of Glasgow. Black told him about the phenomenon known as latent heat, which is involved in change-of-state situations (ice to water, water to steam, or the reverse). However, this merely explained Watt's discovery; it didn't make it possible. It was the discovery itself that showed Watt that he would have to construct a separate cylinder for condensation to save fuel. Watt himself denied any dependence on Black for this invention.

Nevertheless, the line is blurry in this case, for Watt was no unlettered mechanic, and his discovery regarding the behavior of heat was as much theoretical as it was applied. Furthermore, the development of steam power depended on ideas current in the eighteenth and nineteenth centuries regarding notions of atmospheric pressure, which was a lively topic in scientific circles. In addition, Watt's work seems to have been dependent upon the use of scientific method, if not of scientific theory per se; it contains a quantitative, theoretico-experimental aspect that is central to seventeenth-century notions of the investigation of nature.

That, in any case, is the historical picture; in the twentieth century, the dependence of technology and industry upon basic science is a foregone conclusion. No one, for example, can imagine the invention of the transistor without the use of Maxwell's equations (electromagnetic theory). It was during the twentieth century that science, technology, and industry effectively merged into something approaching a unified enterprise, and scientific research lies at the heart of corporate research and development, manufacture, and economic expansion. Even a casual look at the Fortune 500 companies underscores this. Rubber, steel, television, automobile production, the software and information industry—the list goes on and on. The "triumph" of capitalism was hardly the result of Galileo's study of objects being dropped from the Tower of Pisa

(an experiment that was, in any case, never actually per-
formed), but it seems clear enough that once the Western
nations undertook Bacon's program, that of carrying out a "diligent dissection and anatomy of the world," the end result was
the expansion of commercial and technological activity to
every corner of the globe.

Horkheimer and Adorno, correspondingly, make a distinction between a "good" Enlightenment and a "bad" one. The
former is the Age of Reason, the world of Hume and Voltaire,
which gave us our notions of critical analysis. The latter is the
modern obsession with quantification, control, and the domination of the natural world. Human power over nature
increased—we call this "progress"—but so did alienation from
our environment and from the world of meaning and value.
This alienation, in turn, impelled us to seek more power, which
led to more alienation, and so on. "Progress" finally became an
exercise in frustration, what the German sociologist Max
Weber characterized both as the "disenchantment of the
world" and the "iron cage" of industrial society. Underneath it
all, say the Frankfurt writers, is an unconscious neurotic fantasy, the dream of absolute power over everything. In our own
time, it means that cans of Coca-Cola must penetrate into the
most remote villages of Africa, along with satellite television
and Nike running shoes. This is the "skin" I referred to earlier,
the phenomenon by which there is not a square inch of American (or Americanized) life that is not bombarded by commercial messages.

Yet Bacon and Galileo obviously did not live in a world of
endless media blitz and commercial saturation, and if they
could come back to view it, they might conclude that they had
stumbled into a madhouse. The line that runs from Bacon rail-
ing against the dead hand of medieval Scholasticism to America's frenetic, even demented, excitement over, for example,

the "unveiling" of Windows 95 a few years ago is hardly a linear one, and, as I said, cannot be laid at the door of science. The story is not really one of the history of ideas.

What we need to look at, then, is the rise of a corporate commercial culture that science made possible but certainly did not cause. To my mind, the best study of this subject, at least as it pertains to the United States, is William Leach's *Land of Desire: Merchants, Power, and the Rise of a New American Culture*. This, along with James Beniger's *The Control Revolution: Technological and Economic Origins of the Information Society*, provides an excellent picture of the ties between applied science and industrial capitalism, and shows how the values and ideology of marketing and consumerism managed to overwhelm America in the twentieth century. Global corporate hegemony is the furthest point of this whole process, what we have called McWorld. It, and the much-touted information superhighway, are the logical twenty-first century results.

Before 1880, says Leach, the economy of the United States was an agrarian one; most Americans worked on farms. Most markets were regional, most businesses individually owned. In 1870, the average number of workers in any given factory was fewer than ten. In general, the culture was agrarian, republican, and religious.

All of this changed practically overnight. During the years between 1890 and 1930, this nation was transformed by what could be regarded as an alien culture, until this new culture became the dominant one. With lightning speed, new corporations and banks moved into everyday life, accompanied by a world of department stores, chain stores, and mail-order houses (a development brilliantly captured in fiction by Steven Millhauser in his novel *Martin Dressler*). Nor was this development consensual. It was generated by commercial groups in cooperation with other elites committed to accumulating profit on an ever-increasing scale, until this way of viewing the world pushed out any other vision of the good life. The result was a society preoccupied with consumption, a "culture of desire that confused the good life with goods."

Leach acknowledges that this had an Enlightenment ancestry, the ideal of the pursuit of knowledge and "the new"; but capitalism, he says, latched onto this tradition and took it over. The "new" now meant more commodities. The rapid industrialization that took place after 1885 moved with the force of a hurricane, and the exchange of money and goods was the heart of its aesthetic and moral sensibility. Department stores, hotels, and amusement parks began to dot the landscape, and by World War I, buying was seen as the road to happiness. Money became the measure of everything, friendship and religion included.

Part of this movement included the "democratization of desire," the notion that all had equal rights to the world of comfort and luxury, and that this was what life was ultimately about. A commercial aesthetic arose to reinforce this, and after 1880 it could be seen in shop windows, fashion shows, and electric signs, as well as in ads and on billboards. Color, glass, and light were all employed to celebrate the new message. The goal became expanding markets and volume turnover, and cities like New York became "huge havens for brokering." "No country," writes Leach,

> . . . developed the kind of commercial aesthetic, the type of brokering class, the form of institutional circuitry, or the variety of spiritual accommodations as those that emerged in the United States. The United States was the first country in the world to have an economy devoted to mass production, and it was the first to create the mass consumer institutions, and the mass consumer enticements that rose up in tandem to market and sell the mass-produced goods.

These institutions, along with commercial establishments and department-store families such as the Wanamakers, Fields, and Strauses "helped initiate and perpetuate the world's most powerful culture of consumption."

Applied science and technology made all of this possible, as a revolution in the manufacture of industrial goods began. Production of glassware and lamps, for example, rose from 84,000 tons in 1890 to more than 250,000 tons in 1914. The age saw new tools and "continuous-process" machines, along with the exploitation of new energy sources: coal, steam, gas, and electricity. Output speeded up to mass-production levels; major railroad trunk lines were completed by 1895, and the telephone and telegraph increased the rapid movement of goods and money. Giant firms arose: Du Pont (as a manufacturer of explosives), U.S. Steel, Standard Oil. The 500-watt tungsten lamp made possible huge department stores—such as Marshall Field and Macy's—comprising millions of acres of selling space. Electrical sign advertising boomed after 1900, and by 1915 the United States was consuming 50 percent of all the plate glass manufactured in the world. In a trip across America in the mid-1930s, journalist James Rorty wrote that, the Depression notwithstanding, what dominated the country was "the specialized, heavily capitalized, highly speculative and technologically advanced system of dream-manufacture."

This is a world in which "the good" equals goods and "value" equals marketability—the world we now take for granted. As Leach says, the popular belief today is that such a system is liberatory and meets the "real" needs of all human beings.

According to James Beniger, these developments were not only the result of applied science but also of applied scientific *method*, what Max Weber called "rationalization." As Julien Freund defines it (in *The Sociology of Max Weber*), rationalization is "the organization of life through a division and coordi-

nation of activities on the basis of an exact study of men's relations with each other, with their tools and their environment,
for the purpose of achieving greater efficiency and productivi-
ty." What happened, says Beniger, was that the harnessing of
steam power increased the production process and resultant
commodity flow to the point that these threatened to exceed
the capacity of technology to contain them. By 1890, for example, the weekly output of a single blast furnace had risen from
seventy tons to more than one thousand. So the rush was on
to regulate society and economy in terms of objective criteria,
in an effort to manage these events. Thus, the United States
was divided into four standard time zones in 1884; machinery
began to be controlled by feedback devices; and in 1890,
punch cards were used to tabulate census data. Frederick
Winslow Taylor published his *Principles of Scientific Management* in 1911, and Henry Ford inaugurated the modern assem-
bly line in 1913. The 1930s saw the introduction of national
income accounting, econometrics, input-output analysis, linear programming, and statistical decision theory.

Bureaucratic control of mass consumption also arose during this time. We see technologies of trademarks, consumer
packaging, and mass advertising, all of which gave manufac-
turers a way of controlling giant wholesalers and new mass
retailers. Advertising became the scientific management of
public opinion. Rotogravure sections appeared in newspapers
in 1914, neon signs for advertising in 1923, and finally copy
research, test marketing, and, of course, broadcasting. The
development of market feedback techniques (flow of information back to the advertiser) can be dated to 1900. In 1931,
philosopher John Dewey wrote in his seminal work, *Philosophy and Civilization*, "The great scientific revolution is still to
come. It will ensue when men systematically use scientific
procedures for the control of human relationships and the

direction of the social effects of our vast technological machinery. . . ."

And this did come to pass. The scientific-industrial-informational apparatus grew even more dramatically after World War II. The money now spent each year on commercial color, glass, and light, says Leach, runs into the billions, and TV satellites beam commercial desire into every village of the world. We now have 4 billion square feet of land—think of it!—devoted to shopping malls, and the average American is bombarded by phone, mail, and the mass media to buy, buy, buy. The cyclone of business culture swallowed everything up in a consumer ideology, rendering market values the only values. A "stupid, gigantic fraud," the writer Edmund Wilson called it in 1929, and many would argue that things have only gotten worse since then.

Before I start to sound like the Unabomber, however, we have to ask, Is this science, or scientism? When James Clerk Maxwell published "On Governors" in 1868, the first theoretical analysis of control mechanisms, it was, surely, science. When "governors," in the form of mass data-processing-feedback mechanisms, permeate our entire society, we are confronting Horkheimer and Adorno's "bad" Enlightenment. The problem, however—and Horkheimer and Adorno admit it—is that the "good" and the "bad" are not all that separable; historically, they came as a package deal. In fact, as I have said, there is something of a dialectical relationship between the two. Thus, Julien Freund writes that "increasing rationalization and intellectualization transform the dialectics of the inner and the outer world into that of a real void and an imaginary plenitude"—the (empty) land of desire that William Leach describes in such great detail. The dialectical factor is that we cannot live without rational knowledge; but historically speaking, rationality became rationalization. Capitalism overwhelmed science, so to speak, and in the nineteenth century, science was re-created in capitalism's image. In addition, the Industrial Revolution brought with it a rise in population, which then resulted in increasing industrialization, urbanization, and so on, all of which, it can surely be argued, demanded mass production and distribution and the accompanying need for regulation and control. Given enough time, it is doubtful we could have had the "good" Enlightenment without the "bad"; the problem with antiscientific critiques of modern society is that they typically tend to be irrational/romantic, caught up in a rejection of scientism—which, in my view, is justified, but which is also, and perhaps inevitably, a rejection of empirical methodology as well.

This is a horrible choice for us to have to make, and it is why Weber saw Western society as oscillating between rationalization and charisma. The truth, however, is that it is not really a choice we *can* make; and in any case, who would be the "we" who would make it? *All* civilizations are package deals, and the mess we are in unfolded as it did, with science and scientism, consumerism and natural curiosity, hype and the reduction of values to commodity fetishism, all rolled into one. The real question is this: Where is this system going? Where is it likely to be heading, in the twenty-first century, as all of these dialectics play themselves out?

"World-systems," writes historian Janet Abu-Lughod, "do not 'fail'; they 'restructure.' " In particular, she says, when the dynamic of integration, the specific configuration, of a given world system comes apart, something more complicated than simple decline occurs: "the old parts live on and become the materials out of which restructuring develops." But, I would add, they do not live on in quite the same way, or serve quite the same function. This is a subtler approach to the problem of large-scale change than the simple one of "rise and fall," as

Robert Kaplan argues in his article on democracy. But here is the dialectical surprise: If democracy is gradually being transformed into something else, then Europe and the United States will suffer the same fate as earlier civilizations. That is to say, Rome believed that it was the final expression of Greek culture, the republican ideal, whereas we believe that we are the final expression of democracy, that we are are bringing freedom and a better life to all humankind. Kaplan ends his article on a cryptic note, saying that "we are poised to transform ourselves into something perhaps quite different from what we imagine." But given his earlier analysis, it is not that hard to fill in the blank. Just as Rome began by embodying Greek ideals, it looked strikingly different—that is, precisely the opposite—during the period of its collapse. What began as substance survived only as shadow, while the transmuted substance finally contradicted the shadow. As for us, says Kaplan, we shall "sell" democracy to hybrid regimes that will, for economic reasons, take on democratic trappings, while the political reality is something else; and in the process of doing that, we too shall become—are becoming—a hybrid regime. For a zoned-out, stupefied populace, "democracy" will be nothing more than the right to shop, or to choose between Wendy's and Burger King, or to stare at CNN and think that this managed infotainment is actually the news. As I have said, corporate hegemony, the triumph of global democracy/consumerism based on an American model, *is* the collapse of American civilization. So a large-scale transformation *is* indeed going on, but it is one that makes triumph indistinguishable from disintegration.

There are many examples we might give to demonstrate this process; as already noted, higher education is one of the more conspicuous ones. Universities retain an aura of elitism (positively conceived); they are seen as the loci of the most advanced thinking in the land, places where men and women are free to pursue the sciences and the humanities and thus imbibe the highest elements of culture. Latin mottoes adorn the crests of many of these schools, boasting of "light" and "truth." The reality, however, is something very different, as thousands of these institutions have literal or de facto open admissions policies in the name of "democracy." The democratization of desire means that virtually anyone can go to college, the purpose being to get a job; and in an educational world now subsumed under business values, students show up—with administrative blessing—believing that they are consumers who are buying a product. Within this context, a faculty member who actually attempts to enforce the tradition of the humanities as an uplifting and transformative experience, who challenges his charges to think hard about complex issues, will provoke negative evaluations and soon be told by the dean that he had better look elsewhere for a job. Objecting to a purely utilitarian dimension for education is regarded as quaint, and quickly labeled "elitist" (horror of horrors!); but the truth is that there can be no genuine liberal education without such an objection. "Thinking, reading, and art require a cultural space," writes Russell Jacoby in *Dogmatic Wisdom*, "a zone free from the angst of moneymaking and practicality. Without a certain repose or leisure, a liberal education shrivels."

Unfortunately, notes Bill Readings in *The University in Ruins*, this voice is fast disappearing, and he argues that this is due to the phenomenon of globalization, which is undermining the original Enlightenment project. The "good" Enlightenment saw teaching in terms of cultural continuity and the development of critical judgment; in this context, the faculty member was the key player. The "bad," globalized Enlightenment sees education as an expression of the technobureaucratic notion of "excellence," or "total quality management"; therefore, the key player is the administrator. The university may *look* like an institution for the advancement of higher culture, in other words, but its content and organization are corporate, and the result is that the coinage of education is severely debased. ("Another bad effect of commerce," wrote Adam Smith in *Wealth of Nations*, "is that the minds of men are contracted, and rendered incapable of elevation. Education is despised, or at least neglected. . . .")

I had an opportunity to see these tendencies at their worst when I was unexpectedly hired by a trendy "distance learning institute" a few years back. On the face of it—that is, from its published study guides—"Alt. U," as I shall refer to it, sounded quite reputable, and that was what originally drew me in. As I soon discovered, however, the actual educational practice was something else. Like President Clinton, Alt. U had no real identity; it was a kind of corporate creation driven by popular rhetoric and content to identify itself with whatever was academically avant-garde. A large percentage of the students were corporate employees trying to advance their careers by adding Ph.D. after their names, and because the school was 100 percent tuition-driven, these students effectively called the shots. It was thus impossible for Alt. U to enforce (assuming it had even cared about) real academic standards, because this would have threatened its financial base. Hence, an ideology prevailed that *any* academic authority was an "abuse of power," and an instructor who had any notion of serious academic accountability was quickly dropped by the students in favor of one—and there were many—who made very few rigorous intellectual demands. Since mentors had to attract "mentees" in order to survive, it behooved them not to demand very much. As far as I could make out, most applicants were accepted, and the screening interviews were bogus: In the case of the two students I did reject (and this meant they were *really* bad), one was admitted anyway, and the other was reinterviewed twice. Grades for study units completed boiled down basically to Yes and Not Yet, so the student who just kept at it, no matter how inadequate, eventually obtained a Ph.D.

As for the faculty, it was not clear how they had been hired, beyond the fact that they seemed to fit in with the group. Merit was at best a secondary consideration, and a good number of them were embarrassingly unqualified: not only breathtakingly ignorant but aggressively anti-intellectual in their outlook, and contemptuous of any individual expression that violated the group mind. Thus I was ridiculed for using the word *desultory*, and attacked for reading George Steiner. When I once referred to Francis Bacon at a faculty meeting, my colleagues seemed to have no idea whom I was talking about. These "retreats," as they were called, contained large doses of traditional-institution–bashing and had the flavor of cult rituals, binding the group together. The dean took me aside at one point and told me that I would do a lot better at the place if I were to start publicly praising the institution at the retreats— a suggestion reminiscent of the Chinese Cultural Revolution. Reading over student work, I was amazed at how feeble most of it was, how little effort was required of these doctoral candidates, and how easily their work received a passing grade. At one thesis defense I attended, the experimental design was deeply flawed, but the ethos was, Keep your mouth shut. At another, the thesis was little more than a rehash of a famous scholar's work, but again, pointing out lack of originality (originality being the point of a thesis, I always thought) was not acceptable. Many of the theses at Alt. U were purely self-indulgent: A single mother of forty-five, say, would research the topic of the trials and tribulations of single mothers in their mid-forties! The protocol was never to call students "students"; rather, they were "colearners," and in an odd sense, this was accurate, because Alt. U was a classic case of the blind leading the blind.

Alt. U fancied itself a "rebel" organization, expressing a radical rejection of the dominant culture; but if that culture is corporate commercialism, this institution was, in fact, an outstanding representative of it. Its radicalism never took on the real enemy, as it were, but played it safe: radical feminism, deconstruction, postmodernism, systems theory (which, embarrassingly, was never clearly defined), and radical relativism. This was Richard Ellis' "dark side of the left," and it was, at Alt. U, heavily totalitarian. Everything floated in a world of equal values, except for the various dogmas just mentioned, which were the Truth. Some of the faculty were downright eerie, possessing no real center, and espousing "group process" as a kind of salvation. True postmodernists, these were people whose lives were "texts," constantly being "reinvented" to cover up an inherent emptiness. As you might imagine, anyone who disagreed with them, or with this (non)philosophical outlook, was feared, ostracized, and, ultimately, despised.

Multiculturalism—another safe, politically correct position—was worshiped to the point of pathology, and I once witnessed a kind of Moscow trial ritual, in which various faculty members publicly confessed their racist "sins"; some even wept. ("The worst," wrote Yeats, "are full of passionate intensity.") Students and faculty eventually drafted a "diversity" study unit that everyone would be required to take, but only one point of view was represented in its pages. Alt. U approved it enthusiastically, and by the time I left, plans were being drawn up to require every faculty member to demonstrate multicultural credentials—a kind of reverse McCarthyism. I recall the dean saying at one point that it was a drawback when men were decent, because that distracted from the real ideological struggle that the women's movement had to wage.

I left Alt. U with a sense of relief, and never looked back. Yet one thing still haunts me, because the issue here is not one little institute masquerading as an educational institution, joke though the place may have been. In their endless litany of self-praise, the Alt. U faculty frequently boasted that they represented the education of the future; and I fear they just may have been right. For Alt. U may be different only in *degree* from the type of college or university that is evolving in the United States; it may ultimately not be very different in *kind*. My guess is that if you, the reader, are a student or an academic, you recognize elements of your own institution in my description of Alt. U. As Alvin Kernan's career clearly demonstrates, even schools such as Yale and Princeton have fallen victim to grade inflation, consumerism, postmodernism, political correctness, and the like. Thus, philosopher Susan Haack, in her *Manifesto of a Passionate Moderate*, says that she finds in American universities today "a great revolutionary chorus of voices announcing that disinterested inquiry is impossible, that all supposed 'knowledge' is an expression of power, that the concepts of evidence, objectivity, truth, are ideological humbug." As for multiculturalism, she says that attempts to involve more women and African Americans in higher education—attempts that are obviously laudable—"seem to have encouraged the idea that truth, evidence, reason, are tools of their oppression: an idea as tragic as it is bizarre." She cites instances of feminism run amok (the "scholar" who described Newton's *Principia* as a "rape manual," for example), academic arguments that good scholarship and political relevance are and should be identical, assertions that truth and objectivity are myths—the sort of thinking that Alt. U warmly embraced. All of this, as I said, is perfectly congruent with the new postmodern capitalist order. Add to this long-distance, computerized learning, the debasing of academic standards, and the kowtowing of university administrations to market forces (consumerist demands), and you have a situation not terribly removed from the one at Alt. U, if a little less cultish and hysterical. So Alt. U may indeed represent the education of the future; which is to say, in effect, that education *has* no future.

Another area in which Alt. U boasted that it was on the cutting edge was its emphasis on distance learning. This trend, I fear, is a cancer that is spreading throughout the university system and that represents the extreme commercialization of higher education. As of this writing, there are some signs of a backlash against this trend, and historian David Noble has documented some important failures: the rejection, thanks to student and faculty opposition, by the California State University system of a corporate offer (from Microsoft, MCI, Hughes Aircraft, and Fujitsu) to link the CSU campuses in exchange for the right to sell nearly $4 billion worth of high-tech products to students over the next decade, or York University's successful faculty strike in the wake of the administration's attempt at commercial exploitation of on-line education in Canada. But plans for CSU are now being reworked for a different form of corporate partnership, and UCLA has created the Home Education Network, a for-profit company headed by a former UCLA vice-chancellor. My guess is that the setbacks are temporary, inasmuch as the players are too powerful to be held off indefinitely: Apple, IBM, Dell, the cable companies, Microsoft, Disney, Viacom, and so on. As at Alt. U, what we are getting is education watered down and converted to a commodity—a "degraded, shadow cybereducation," as David Noble calls it, in which content will be shaped by media businesspeople. Thus, eminent visionary Mike Leavitt, governor of Utah, proclaimed that "an institution of higher education will become a little like a local television station," while an equally eminent visionary, Dean Marvin Loflin of the University of Colorado at Denver, who in 1998 was planning to hire nonprofessional "teaching associates" to teach on-line courses, declared, "I'm prepared to make over the whole infra-structure of higher education."

The process of market values invading every area of our lives, of course, is hardly limited to education. The media is another key area. Traditionally, we have regarded it as the bastion of a free society. One thinks of Benjamin Franklin and Thomas Paine, of Emile Zola shouting, "*J'accuse!*" in the Drey-fus Affair, or perhaps of Woodward and Bernstein as recently as 1974. What are the press and the media now but institu-tions designed to generate an endless stream of minute, use-less information as a form of news-entertainment ("nuzak")? Consider the so-called feeding frenzy that broke out in Jan-uary 1998, when President Clinton was accused of having some sort of sexual relationship with a White House intern, Monica Lewinsky. Not only was the ratio of hype to factual content something that bordered on infinity but, in a parody of itself, television also began to air programs on the subject of its own hyperfrenetic coverage. As in the case of the corporate university, there is a tremendous amount of energy that is evi-dent in all of this; the media packaging of the whole event made one feel that exciting things were going on. But actual-ly, very little was going on, because the fact content of the news was almost nonexistent; rather, the coverage dealt with allegations and the interpretations consequent upon them. As a few observers pointed out, it was really the continuation of the O. J. Simpson trial, but with different dramatis person-ae. So we have an educational system that is not really about education, and a press that is not really about the reportage of the news.

When we look at where we have come since the Renaissance, we see the expansion of secular and scientific knowledge to the point that it has made the technocommercial world of the twentieth century possible, from the endless "cold calls" one receives for hundreds of superfluous products and services to Nike's exploitation of women and children in Indonesia. The Enlightenment turned into its opposite, leaving us with James Beniger's "control revolution," William Leach's "land of desire," and Ben Barber's "McWorld," all of which, in turn, evoked a series of disturbed responses: the New Age, deconstruction, Gaia, the Unabomber, sentimental ecology, religious fundamentalism, Deepak Chopra-ism, "education" along the lines of Alt. U, and so on. Pushed far enough, yang becomes yin, and brilliance turns into bullshit.

"Vital kitsch," the promotion of commercial energy at the expense of genuine content, of real substance, will be the reality for most Americans in the twenty-first century, in one form or another, and it will be fueled by the globalization process. Most of those who claim to oppose the world of corporate sci-tech consumerism will themselves become commodities, making the round of the talk shows and selling "soul" or "green earth" or "total health" as the latest commercial fad. Their ideas will become slogans on T-shirts; they will become the trendy spearheads of the latest form of "liberation," soon to be forgotten for the next fad on the horizon. John Updike captures the larger landscape of all this in his 1998 collection of stories, *Bech at Bay*, when he has his protagonist say:

> Greedy authors, greedy agents, brainless book chains with their Vivaldi-riddled espresso bars, publishers owned by metallurgy conglomerates operated by glacially cold bean-counters in Geneva. And meanwhile language . . . is becoming the mellifluous happy-talk of Microsoft and Honda,

corporate conspiracies that would turn the world into one
big pinball game for child-brained consumers. . . .

Does the reader doubt the accuracy of this description for a
moment? Disney, now linked to McDonald's in a cross-licensing
partnership, organizes play around its own version of American
values, giving our children toys, dolls, coloring books, and
images that are burned into their brains. Our kids are hooked
on this stuff no less fiercely than by the added nicotine in
cigarettes and the ads that got them smoking in the first place.
Our entire consciousness, our intellectual-mental life, is being
Starbuckized, condensed into a prefabricated designer look in
a way that is reminiscent of that brilliant, terrible film, *The
Invasion of the Body Snatchers* (a great metaphor for our time).
We are becoming a nation of "pods," for there is very little that
can resist the American commercial process, and if something
does make it into the public eye, it is almost by definition
devoid of the opaque richness, the *inaccessibility*, that things of
real quality inevitably have. "Business," wrote the American
essayist John Jay Chapman in 1898 (*Practical Agitation*), "has
destroyed the very knowledge in us of all other natural forces
except business."

Writing about the subject of handicrafts, Rosemary Hill, the
British potter and art critic, comments: "To make objects by
hand in an industrial society, to work slowly and uneconomi-
cally against the grain, is to offer, however inadvertently, a critique of that society." This is a good description of the
principles embodied in the monastic option, but it needs to be
construed in a much larger cultural sense than handicrafts.
Craftsmanship should apply to all of life, and since its core
value is the work itself—the very opposite of the purpose of
American corporate consumerism—those genuinely commit-

ted to the monastic option need to stay out of the public eye; to do their work quietly, and deliberately avoid media attention. Indeed, a Taoist rule of thumb might be that if the larger culture knows about it, then it's not the real thing. We are now ready, then, to ask, Who is this new monastic "class," and what activities might it reasonably pursue?

THE MONASTIC OPTION IN
THE TWENTY-FIRST CENTURY

There are people in the world all the time who know. . . .
But they keep quiet. They just move about quietly, saving
the people who know they are in the trap. And then, for the
ones who have got out, it's like coming around from chloro-
form. They realise that all their lives they've been asleep and
dreaming. And then it's their turn to learn the rules and the
timing. And they become the ones to live quietly in the
world, just as human beings might if there were only a few
human beings on a planet that had monkeys on it for inhab-
itants, but the monkeys had the possibility of learning to
think like human beings. But in the poor sad monkeys' damaged brains there's a knowledge half-buried. They sometimes think that if they only knew how, if only they could
remember properly, then they could get out of the trap, they
could stop being zombies.

— Doris Lessing,
Briefing for a Descent into Hell

One of my intentions in writing *The Twilight of American Culture* was to create a kind of guidebook for disaffected Americans who feel increasingly unable to fit into this society, and
who also feel that the culture has to change if it is to survive. I

was hoping, in other words, to offer something by way of a road map to anyone who is interested in orienting him- or herself to the events of the new century and in finding meaning in a disintegrating culture. I have argued that we are in the grip of structural forces that are the culmination of a certain historical process, so a major change is not likely to be quick or dramatic; but individual shifts in lifeways and values may just possibly act as a wedge that would serve as a counterweight to the world of schlock, ignorance, social inequality, and mass consumerism that now defines the American landscape. At the very least, these "new monks," or native expatriates, as one might call them, could provide a kind of record of authentic ways of living that could be preserved and handed down, to resurface later on, during healthier times.

How might this preservation and transmission take place? Although the public face of American civilization in the twenty-first century will be vital kitsch, a tiny fraction of the population will be interested in doing something very different with their lives, going "underground," as it were, so that their contributions cannot be co-opted as slogans and drained of content. I am not talking about putting the Great Books on CD-ROM (eventually to be buried in a time capsule, I suppose), or on the Net; these things have already been done, and they don't amount to much, because the Great Books program is really a way of life, not a database. Of course, the preservation of a "database" did work the last time around, during the Dark Ages; but that was a time in which information was relatively scarce, and so its recovery was all the more dramatic. This time around, we are *drowning* in information; hence, what is required is that it be *embodied*, preserved through ways of living. If *this* can get passed down, our cultural heritage may well serve as a seed for a subsequent renaissance. When, over one hundred years from now, that renaissance takes place, and starts to inform itself with the latest round of monastic preservation, the last dozen decades or so may be seen by the majority of Americans, not just by 2 percent of them, for what they were: a *caricature* of culture, a parade of mental theme parks.

The job of preservation and transmission at the present time thus consists in creating "zones of intelligence" in a private, local way, and then deliberately keeping them out of the public eye. This is not about "fifty ways to save the earth," "voluntary simplicity," or some program of trendy ascetic activities. Nor does it involve anything showy and dramatic, and virtually anyone reading this book is capable of making an effort in this direction. As Ray Bradbury has one of the "book people" in *Fahrenheit 451* say, "The most important single thing we had to pound into ourselves is that we were not important. . . . We're nothing more than dust jackets for books, of no significance otherwise." There should, in short, be nothing heroic about the monastic option; an individual is a vehicle for a healthy culture, but it is a project that by definition has no glory attached to it, and offers no immediate payoff beyond a personal one. Applying this to the field of higher education, for example, the "new monastic individual" might take his or her cue from the sociologist Todd Gitlin, who asserts that the point of the nearly forgotten liberal arts is to counter a "high-velocity, reckless, and lightweight culture whose main value is marketability." This value, he goes on, cannot tell us who we are, because it cannot teach us anything about what really endures. Hence, faculty members in the liberal arts need to say something like the following to their lightweight, consumer-oriented students (or, for that matter, their tediously ideological ones):

"Amid the weightless fluff of a culture of obsolescence, here is Jane Austen on psychological complication, Balzac on the pecuniary squeeze. Here is Dostoyevsky wrestling with God, Melville with nothingness, Douglass with slavery. Here is Rembrandt's religious inwardness, Mozart's exuberance, Beethoven's longing. In a culture of chaff, here is wheat."

Eschewing the trendy path, and making your students work— that is, think—might mean losing your job; but if you are committed to the monastic option (or, for that matter, to having any sort of meaning in your life at all), you let the chips fall where they may.

I shall talk about other examples of the monastic option below, but I wish first to say something about the "guerrilla" nature of this way of life. In order to grasp the nature of "monastic" psychology, we need to understand the concept of nomadic consciousness, or what might be called "spiritual nomadism." I want to consider the possibility that every age has an extremely small fraction of people who go their own way without making a big production out of it: not Jean-Paul Sartre, but Boris Vian; not Goethe, but Heinrich von Kleist; not Martin Heidegger, but Ludwig Wittgenstein. These are bohemians with a small *b*, in other words; their work breaks with fixed forms, and it is often about the idea of breaking with fixed forms. Yet they don't try to elevate their iconoclasm into a movement, a new fixed form. In his book *Class*, Paul Fussell calls this group "Class X," but since this group, for the most part, has very little in common with Generation X, I am going to substitute the acronym NMI, the new monastic individual. NMIs, says Fussell, make up the class of people that belong to no class, have no membership in a hierarchy. They form a kind of "unmonied aristocracy," free of bosses, supervision, and what is typically called "work." They work very hard, in fact, but as they love their work and do it for its intrinsic interest, this work is not much different from play. In the context of contemporary American culture, such people are an anomaly, for they have no interest in the world of business success and mass consumerism. Their credo, if it could be formulated at all, most closely approximates a haiku by the seventeenth-century Japanese poet Bashō:

> Journeying through the world
> To and fro, to and fro
> Cultivating a small field.

This is, of course, the aristocracy (which is actually a nonaristocracy) referred to by E. M. Forster; and to his assessment of this group, Forster adds the observation that with such people knocking about, "the experiment of earthly life cannot be dismissed as a failure. But it may well be hailed as a tragedy, the tragedy being that no device has been found by which these private decencies can be transmitted to public affairs." And Forster is right, except that if nomadic behavior *could* be so transmitted, it would no longer be nomadic; and in addition, some sort of transmission may still go on without a "device"—that is, without any form of institutionalization. NMIs may, in other words, have a profound historical impact, but without intending it or even being aware of it. At the very least, they leave behind, by the example of their lives, the knowledge that people can, in fact, do this, live the "nomadic" life.

The guerrilla nature of spiritual nomadism received one of its finest expositions in a book by Gilles Deleuze and Félix Guattari entitled *Nomadology*, which makes a distinction between what the authors call "smooth" and "striated" space. This difference can best be appreciated by comparing the games of chess and Go. Such a comparison was in fact made three decades ago by Scott Boorman in *The Protracted Game:*

A Wei-Chi Interpretation of Maoist Revolutionary Strategy.
Boorman argued that Mao Zedong was able to defeat the
Kuomintang because he was using a Go (*wei-chi* in Chinese)
strategy while the Kuomintang sought, à la chess, to stake out
and occupy—that is, striate—territory. In the language of
Deleuze and Guattari, chess pieces are "coded"; they have an
internal nature, distinctive moves, like soldiers in an army.
They function in a structural way, in combinations, mounting
pressure on a particular point so as to create a breakthrough,
for example. The victory—death of the king—is an all-or-nothing
proposition. This is the logic of the state.

Go is an entirely different affair. Like members of a guerrilla army, Go pieces are anonymous, simple arithmetical units
(identical black and white stones). They have no intrinsic prop-
erties, but only situational ones, functioning by insertion, for
example, or encirclement. A Go piece can destroy an entire
constellation in a single moment, whereas chess requires a
diachronic strategy. Victory is relative, rather than absolute, in
Go; it follows the logic of the pasture (*nomos* in Greek) rather
than the state (*polis*). Striated space requires endless vigilance
and defense; smooth space, on the other hand, is slippery.
When threatened, an object in smooth space simply goes
somewhere else. Since this space is about nonestablishment,
nonterritory, there is nothing to defend.

The conflict between smooth and striated space can also be
seen in the history of science and art, as well as in politics. Cal-
culus, say Deleuze and Guattari, began as a nomadic science.
With its "unruly" notions of the limit and the infinitesimal, its
focus was almost completely on process, on becoming. State
mathematicians sought to eliminate such nomadic notions and
instead impose static rules upon them, which they did. In the
same way, the state needs hydraulic systems (for irrigation, for
example), but it needs to control the flow by means of pipes

and conduits so as to prevent turbulence. The state always seeks to control the ambulatory and the heuristic, and this can be seen in everything from music to cathedral building. Nothing must be vagabond; nothing must just follow the natural meandering of things. Nomadic thought, on the other hand, dwells in the midregions, the grasslands and the steppes. The model is that of a tribe in the desert, of relays and intermezzos, rather than that of a universal subject. In the nomadic mind, say Deleuze and Guattari, the tent is not tied to a territory, but to an itinerary. Points are reached, only to be left behind. The road to truth is always under construction; the going is the goal. As the French anthropologist Pierre Clastres once put it, "Thought is loyal to itself only when it moves *against the incline.*" And this is the great legacy of the "good" Enlightenment tradition—that it is always moving against the grain, always asking us to look deeper into life.

So Fussell's NMIs do not form any identifiable group or class, and if you posted a notice trying to organize a meeting of them, the real ones wouldn't show, because they have better things to do. An NMI doesn't participate in anything that can be labeled an "ism." She might be an independent woman, but never a feminist; he might do environmental work, but keep his distance from Greenpeace. For an NMI knows the historical irony, of how movements start out with vibrant critical energy and wind up as the new (oppressive) orthodoxies, complete with texts, heroes, and slogans. So this person keeps in mind the admonition of Wittgenstein—"The true philosopher is not a member of any community of ideas"—without becoming a Wittgensteinian. As a result, the NMI is the purist embodiment of the human spirit.

I intend to give a few examples or case studies of monastic activity below, but the reader should be aware of the paradoxical issue involved in this: If the activity is undertaken expressly to *be* monastic activity, then it really isn't one, and will probably do more harm than good. This raises the question of how such activity can actually serve as a vehicle for the preservation of culture during the coming dark age, and, as already indicated, it may not. History is capricious and nonlinear; it doesn't promise *anything*. What we *can* say, however, is that there will be no such preservation *without* this activity, so it makes sense, following Bashō's advice, to "cultivate a small field." What I am offering here, once again, is not Utopia, but, hopefully, realistic optimism.

Given the cultural degradation that is integral to the transformation Robert Kaplan describes—the rise of global corporate hegemony, erosion of democracy, moronization of the American public, and so on—there are a number of fronts on which the monastic option can proceed. One of the most important categories here is that of exposing the emptiness of the corporate/commercial way of life. A good example of this is the twenty-year "career" of David Barsamian, who runs a weekly one-hour program on National Public Radio called "Alternative Radio." The program provides a forum for information and analyses that are typically ignored by the major, corporate-controlled media. Featured speakers include folks such as Frances Fox Piven, who speaks candidly about welfare (it's a nonissue, a minute fraction of the national budget); Jeff Cohen, who exposes the distortions of mainstream media reporting; and Noam Chomsky, among many others. In 1996, John Cavanna, codirector of the Institute for Policy Studies in Washington, D.C., lectured on the topic "Global Economic Apartheid," showing how the corporate project of turning the world into a giant shopping mall was homogenizing the planet and enabling companies to deny foreign workers their rights, and pay them 5 to 10 percent of what they would earn in the United States. Etc.

I recently interviewed Barsamian in Boulder, Colorado, and was impressed by the shoestring quality of the whole operation. Barsamian sends his tapes to radio stations for free; it costs them absolutely nothing to air these lectures—if they have the courage to do so. Alternative Radio survives entirely by listener purchases of program tapes and transcripts, even though, I would guess, the regular listening audience is not terribly large. Barsamian's lifestyle is far from luxurious, and corporations are not offering him any funding. But he hasn't missed a meal in twenty years, and he gets to spend his time doing what he cares about. Were you thinking there was a better way to live?

Alternative Radio, of course, will probably not manage to derail the globalization process, but it suggests that a noncommercial way of life is possible. This doesn't mean returning to the agrarian days of antebellum America, but it does mean getting free of a world dominated by market and utilitarian values—one of the greatest contributions an NMI can make. Hopefully, it will remain small scale. The day you see Barsamian on "Larry King Live," you can be sure Alternative Radio has lost its edge.

A second example in this category is an obscure Canadian magazine called *Adbusters*, published in Vancouver, British Columbia. This journal is dedicated to ridiculing and exposing a life built around the notion that buying things is the key to happiness. It regularly caricatures popular ads for cigarettes, cars, alcohol, and so on in ways that are quite hilarious, and it hammers home the idea that a life based on commodities is bankrupt. Here is a poem from the Winter 1998 issue:

> Like everyone else, I had it backwards
> Now I know that acquiring things can
> never fill an emptiness within

> I wonder if there is any hope for others
> trapped inside the culture of acquisition
> I feel like an escapee . . .

It ain't exactly Keats, but literature is not the purpose here.

I am also impressed that *Adbusters* is aware of the potential danger of anticonsumer fetishism. Hence their willingness to publish the following anonymous letter to the editor in the Spring 1998 issue:

> A friend of mine said something today which jolted me. She had read your magazine and came up to tell me how cool it was and she kept going on about the "alternative" image of the magazine, its "coolness," the "cool pictures," etc. . . .

> It seems she had bought into *Adbusters'* "rebel-alternative" image. Instead of probing us to think for ourselves, *Adbusters* runs the risk of altering the present mindlessness into another kind of empty-brain syndrome—except this time you're the programmer.

I would guess that the worldwide circulation of *Adbusters* is relatively minuscule; its chances of overtaking *Fortune* or *Business Week* probably aren't too great. Will it defeat the consumer society? It doesn't look that way. Is it worth publishing? Absolutely. What's the worst thing that could happen to it? It gets bought out and repackaged by Time Warner.

Another example of monastic opposition to corporate domination, and one that has, in fact, received a great deal of media attention, is the work of the rebel filmmaker Michael Moore. Moore began his career in 1976 with an alternative newspaper in Flint, Michigan, which he ran for ten years, while also hosting a weekly radio show, "Radio Free Flint." All of this was

penny-ante stuff; Moore never took a salary of more than fifteen thousand dollars in any given year. Then in the late eight-
ies, Moore made a low-budget film about General Motors
closing its factories in Flint and throwing thirty thousand people—20 percent of Flint's total population—out of work at a
time when profits were up and GM was actually doing quite
well. As the social structure of the town collapsed, Moore documented his attempt to get Roger Smith, then CEO of GM,
to come to Flint and see the effects of what he had done. The
resulting film, entitled *Roger & Me*, released in 1989, raked in
more than $25 million at the box office, making it the highest-
grossing documentary ever made, and earning it a number of
prestigious awards. In the final days of production, Moore
offered to sell the rights to PBS for ten thousand dollars, which
turned it down because "it wasn't funny enough." In fact, the
film is hilarious; and Warner Bros., seeing its potential, bought
the distribution rights for $3 million. Moore wound up with a
nice corner office in the Warner Bros. building, near Rocke-
feller Center in New York.

What is *Roger & Me* about? The story line concerns an over-
weight, unattractive guy trying to interview an expensively
dressed, powerful captain of industry. In the course of this
odyssey, we watch corporate lackeys save their skins by giving
dishonest or bureaucratic answers; see the town of Flint fall
apart, as desperate ex-GM employees do anything they can to
survive; watch these people being evicted from their homes
during Christmas week, while Roger Smith delivers a "religious," "uplifting" peace-on-earth speech to GM executives
and coworkers at the annual Christmas party. Above all, we
see Smith up close, when Moore finally does manage to con-
front him at a stockholders' meeting and ask him to visit Flint.
Smith tells him that he's not interested; effectively, that he

doesn't care about Flint and is not willing to be accountable for his actions. This is the climax of the film, for the viewer gets to see who is really unattractive here. In the two or three years after *Roger & Me* was released, GM laid off another 74,000 employees.

What, Moore has asked in public interviews, is the difference between the terrorism of the Oklahoma City bombing (1995) and the terrorism practiced by GM in Flint? Why, he adds, don't we let GM sell crack cocaine, since the company manages to destroy communities just as effectively. In a subsequent (1998) film entitled *The Big One*, Moore interviews the CEO of Nike, Phil Knight, who admits to employing fourteen-year-olds in the corporation's Indonesian factories. He reveals that he is unwilling to help anybody; that his whole life is about money and power. From a "monastic" point of view, it is important for American audiences to see such people close-up.

What about Moore? Has success spoiled *him*? It certainly has the potential to do so—*The Big One* is distributed by Miramax—and it seems to me that he is going to have to be very careful not to become a commodity of an "alternative" sort. But to date, Moore's record remains extremely good. He set up the Center for Alternative Media to subsidize independent filmmakers and liberal social causes, has resisted attempts by Warner Bros. to get him to make slick, commercial films; and pulls out his checkbook and gives money to fledgling filmmakers when the occasion arises. Much to his credit, the rich and powerful dislike and avoid him, and his TV program, *TV Nation*, which ran two short seasons, was finally kicked off the air. Moore considers this a badge of honor, saying that this kind of rejection is a sure sign that is doing something right. Indeed, to get rejected by men like Roger Smith and Phil

Knight would almost certify one as an NMI (if not, more simply, as a decent human being). Asked by *Newsweek* whether
he thought realistic options for change existed, Moore replied
that the odds weren't great, but that the challenge was to
develop a democratic economic system. He went on:

> It's not called capitalism and it's not called socialism. A sys-
> tem that on one hand is fair to everyone—everyone gets a
> decent slice of the pie—but on the other hand doesn't stifle
> creativity, that encourages an individual to excel and to help
> us all progress as a society. That's the kick, right there.

As it turns out, such an experiment was attempted in the
twentieth century by a great and little-known NMI by the name
of José María Arizmendi, who began his career as a student
priest in Spain. Arizmendi was a journalist during the Spanish
Civil War, and when the latter was over, he returned to his studies. His goal was to try to balance the needs of community with
individual property rights; to find a middle path, in other words,
between capitalism and socialism. In 1941 he was assigned to
the Basque parish of Mondragón, and in 1956, after years of
teaching, preaching, and private study, he started a factory with
five other men in the village. It was called Ulgor, and it manufactured paraffin heaters and cookers. Eventually, this led to the
foundation of a savings bank, a training school, and a network
of industrial cooperatives, all worker-owned, and having a salary
differential, top to bottom, of 3:1. By 1987, there were more
than one hundred cooperatives, twenty thousand workers, and
a salary differential of 6:1, quite remarkable in a world of corporations with differentials of 400:1 or more. The co-ops follow
a principle of verticality when it comes to expertise, but a horizontal political structure of one person, one vote. Despite a
strike that occurred in 1974, the Mondragón experiment has

been very successful. In 1986, when unemployment in the Basque region exceeded 25 percent, the Mondragón co-ops added five hundred new jobs.

As for Arizmendi, he appears to have been nearly egoless, resisting attempts to turn him into a modern saint. He deliberately stayed out of the strike in 1974, so as not to influence the negotiations by his reputation, and resisted attempts to honor him and personalize the movement he had founded. He was, in the words of one biographer, "allergic to all isms . . . including cooperativism." "Isms imprison and oppress us," wrote Arizmendi; "To live is to renew oneself."

Of course, people couldn't let it alone. Planeloads of American sociologists arrived, trying to distill the "formula" of Mondragón (they failed); when Don José died, plaques and icons sprung up everywhere, and hagiographical biographies followed as a matter of course. All of this, Arizmendi would have deplored, for it represents the antithesis of his nonphilosophy. "We build the road as we travel," he was fond of saying, quoting a line from the Spanish poet Antonio Machado.

A second possible arena for monastic activity is that of alternative education, but please be clear that by this phrase, I do not mean the sort of schooling that was popular in the sixties and seventies, designed to break with the traditional curriculum. As already noted, the California-style "create your own degree program" has proven to be little more than a joke, granting degrees for private indulgences, trendy ideologies, and often promoting a "distance" (computerized) learning that fits in all too well with the new global economy. This is consumer education at its worst. I am referring, instead, to experiments that attempt to *preserve* the Enlightenment tradition, not discard it (which the aforementioned institutions often do as a bizarre matter of pride).

One of the most remarkable experiments in this genre is the Clemente Course in the Humanities, founded by Earl

Shorris in 1994, and described in some detail by Shorris in *Harper's* magazine in September 1997, and in his book *New American Blues*. The whole project is a gem of monastic subversion, combining, as it does, a blow for the Enlightenment tradition and against the culture of poverty that has destroyed the lower class. Shorris had been working on a book on poverty, and he came to the conclusion that the convergence of numerous forces—hunger, drugs, landlords, the police, and so on—enclosed the poor in a kind of negative psychic field, a "surround of force" from which they could not escape, similar to the "fog" that I observed in the charter school in Washington, D.C. This prevented them from becoming political, so that they had no way to fight back. One prison inmate suggested to Shorris that the only way out was for the poor to learn "the moral life of downtown"—that is, the world of the humanities, because this is where people learned to reflect. This remark set off a lightbulb for Shorris, giving him the idea for an experimental course in the humanities for the long-term underclass—a course based on the University of Chicago Great Books program, which had, decades before, been pioneered by Robert Maynard Hutchins.

In order to qualify for Shorris' course, an individual had to be able to read a tabloid newspaper and have a household income of less than 150 percent of the Census Bureau's official poverty threshold. The course would provide students with bus and subway fare. In terms of recruitment, Shorris made presentations at various settlement houses around New York City, mostly to blacks and Latinos, some of whom wouldn't shake his hand, and/or were sullen or wary. His pitch? "You've been cheated. Rich people," Shorris told them, "learn the humanities." Poor people don't. The humanities are a way of learning to reflect on the world, a key to becoming political, getting power. That, said Shorris, is the difference between the haves and the have-nots in this society. His audiences heard him; eventually, thirty people signed up.

Meanwhile, Shorris was spectacularly unsuccessful in trying to raise money for the project. A bit did come in, but, as Shorris told his audience at a lecture he gave at the University of Washington on 20 January 1998, most of the foundations he approached laughed hysterically when he outlined the project to them. This kind of dismissal is important, because it is a likely indicator that what is being proposed is true monastic work. If your idea is attracting major corporate subsidy, then you are probably doing something terribly wrong. Like Barsamian and Moore, Shorris wound up paying for much of the project out of pocket.

In any case, the first Clemente class included four ex-cons, three homeless people, one drug addict, and one person who was dying of AIDS. As Shorris put it—and presumably his corporate nonbackers put it to him—"Why should they care about fourteenth-century Italian painting or truth tables or the death of Socrates?"

But care they did. They identified with Plato's Parable of the Cave, and saw education as a way out. They were concerned about Athens' victimization of Socrates. They marveled at the Egyptian galleries at the Metropolitan Museum of Art. After each class was over, they gathered in clusters outside in the cold, and debated problems in logic. They were stunned by the message of the *Nicomachean Ethics*. About half of them—fourteen out of thirty—fell by the wayside, due to AIDS, pregnancy, clinical depression, or other problems, but sixteen made it through. One year later, ten of these were attending four-year colleges or going to a professional school.

It is encouraging to note that Shorris took the attitude that political correctness is completely misguided. As he writes in

New American Blues, the true division in education is between
a market-driven culture and the humanities, not between an
Asian poem and a European one. "The humanities," he states,

> will always be heavily influenced by the work of the dead
> white men of Europe, for they have been history's trouble-
> makers, the fomenters of revolutions and inventions, the
> impetus of change, the implacable enemies of the silence in
> which humanity perishes. No other great body of work
> invites criticism or denies loneliness to the same extent, and
> no other body of work in all the history of the world led to
> politics, with its still astonishing notion of autonomy.

This reminds me of an incident that captures his commitment. I was talking to Shorris after his lecture at the University of Washington in 1998, when he was approached by two
men around thirty years of age wearing "Guatemalan freedom
fighter outfits," or something akin to that. One said to Shorris:
"Why are you teaching Western culture, which is oppressive
and warlike? You should be teaching tribal and native lore,
which is gentle and liberatory." Shorris gave him a gentle, and
hopefully liberatory, reply: "I don't see," he said, "how teaching
people to reflect on the meaning of their lives can be oppressive." And with that, he turned away.

About a year later, I ran across a paragraph in Nathan
McCall's remarkable book, *Makes Me Wanna Holler*, that
reminded me of this exchange. The passage shows how central
"dead white males" remain to everybody's freedom, and gives
the lie to the notion that studying Western civilization is for the
privileged alone. McCall, a black journalist for the *Washington
Post*, who did three years for armed robbery, describes how a
group of prison inmates formed a Western civ discussion
group:

We debated theories of the major philosophers: Spinoza, Kant, Hegel, Kierkegaard, and Sartre, among others. We dissected dualism, pantheism, and existentialism, and discussed questions such as: How can you appreciate good until you've known evil? Does essence precede existence, or does existence precede essence? Sometimes, during those conversations, I was struck by the strangeness of former robbers, drug dealers, and murderers standing in the middle of a prison yard, debating the heaviest philosophical questions of all time.

What would ruin the Clemente Course? Alas, institutionalization, which is well under way. Once unable to obtain funding, the Clemente Course is now pulling in significant financial support from the U.S. Department of Education, various foundations, and state commissions on the humanities. The project has since become a program run by Bard College; there are seven such courses in the United States now, and under Bard's direction, the CC will be expanding to nearly fifty sites in the next five years, including branches in Canada, Mexico, and France. The natural fear is that such success will turn the CC into a trendy gimmick. Shorris, in fact, was even approached to do a movie about the CC—very likely along the lines of movies like *To Sir with Love*, or that absurd Michelle Pfeiffer film, *Dangerous Minds*. (Shorris, to his credit, rejected the idea.)

Another monastic experiment in alternative education is the North Carolina Abecedarian Project, which provided impoverished children with first-class educational child care from birth to age five. As opposed to the gloomy predictions of that infamous 1990s book *The Bell Curve*, the Abecedarian Project managed to generate significant and stable gains in IQ levels. But these gains are really a symptom of something more important, a social responsiveness that children develop in such a high-quality context, enabling them to absorb information from adults. A similar project, the Michigan High/Scope Perry Preschool Study, tracked roughly sixty poor black children, who had been given a quality education at age three and four, to their twenty-seventh year. It turned out that only 7 percent of these subjects had been arrested five times or more, as compared with 35 percent for a control group; in dramatically higher proportion, they had decent incomes, owned homes, were not on welfare, had stable marriages, and so on.

Of course, the notion of a crucial "target window" for children up to the age of three got a lot of media coverage in 1997, which included a special issue of *Newsweek* devoted to the subject, and an hour-long television program featuring Bill and Hillary Clinton. All of this was froth, and it quickly faded from public attention as the media went on to the next "hot topic." Despite the media blitz, however, experiments such as High/Scope and Abecedarian might survive, in that the real monastic crux here is a qualified teacher working one-on-one with an infant. Becoming open to life and learning, rather than being trapped in what Shorris calls the "surround of force," then emerges as a real possibility.

Switching to the high school level, an outstanding example of monastic activity is the project of a history teacher, Will Fitzhugh, who in 1987 started a quality journal of history research papers written by high school students from around the world. *The Concord Review* has a high-quality feel to it, and it covers topics ranging from the Elgin Marbles to the My Lai massacre. The writing is very sophisticated, and other high school teachers have begun using the essays in their own classes as examplars. To develop and maintain the journal, Fitzhugh spent eighty thousand dollars, his entire life savings, while most foundations rejected his appeal for funds on the grounds that the *Review* was "elitist" because it accepted only the best work. (How is it, in the United States, that excellence in sports is celebrated, while excellence in scholarship is considered elitist?) In fact, Fitzhugh's only criterion for publication is quality, and he is not afraid to reject politically correct work if it is second-rate. In 1993, and again in 1995, he had to suspend publication for lack of funds, but the journal finally prevailed and was ultimately awarded $85,000 from the Argosy Foundation. Although one "elitist" journal can do only so much, it has sent the message to many students that it is okay to achieve, to have intellectual talent and exercise it. As an article in the *Boston Globe* (20 December 1992) pointed out, the journal encourages teenagers to have high expectations for themselves. It has made inroads against the common American high school ethos that "dumb is cool," in part because it is, in all likelihood, the only published history journal in the world devoted to the academic work of secondary school students. The articles are not merely scholarly; they also pulse with energy, reflecting the passion of their writers for the subjects at hand. Although *The Concord Review* has received raves from scholars, total subscribers number five hundred—a nice monastic figure.

Of course, the intellectual poverty of American high schools has not gone unnoticed by many parents and teenagers, and there is by now a loose institutional underground movement known as home schooling, which is quite extensive, involving anywhere from 700,000 to 1.2 million children nationwide. Part of it, I regret to say, is fueled by Christian fundamentalists who don't want their children exposed to Darwin or anything that conflicts with their beliefs. But a significant percentage involves parents who are being "monastic" on behalf of their children: They cannot afford to send them to private schools, but they recognize that the public school system runs the gamut from useless to dangerous. A 1998 study of more than twenty thousand home-schooled students revealed that these children perform significantly better than public or private school students on standardized tests (median scores in the seventieth and eightieth percentiles), and that at least 25 percent of these students were studying at a level one or more grades above normal for their age. The study may be somewhat flawed, in that a bigger factor here may be family background, which involves a higher degree of education than the parents of non-home-schooled children. Still, it is interesting that so many well-educated adults would see home schooling as the best way for their kids to learn anything.

My own acquaintance with the home-schooling movement, if I can digress for a moment, is a personal, rather than an institutional, one. A few years ago, I unexpectedly received a call from a woman who wanted me to tutor her thirteen-year-old daughter, Sarah, in philosophy and literature. Sarah, it turned out, was quite precocious, having been tutored by her mother up to that point, thus having been able to avoid the numbing effects of public education. I started her out, in any case, with some poems: Keats' "On First Looking into Chapman's Homer" and Leigh Hunt's "Abou Ben Adhem." Side by side, Sarah and I read the text of Plato's *Meno*, and then discussed what knowledge was, and where it came from. On another occasion, I got her to memorize Lewis Carroll's "Jabberwocky," and to write an essay on "Why I Like George Gershwin."

One day I said to Sarah, "We've been studying the Greeks for a few weeks now; let's look at their language." I took a sentence from Patricia Storace's book *Dinner with Persephone*. Storace quotes the line "*Arkhe tou paramythiou, kalispera sas.*"

"You actually know some of these words," I said to Sarah. "Let's start with *arkhe*. Can you think of a word in English that is similar?"

"Ark," said Sarah.

"Right you are," I replied. "Anything else?"

"Archaeology?" she asked tentatively.

"Full marks. *Arkhe* means 'begins.' The word is about origins. How about *paramythiou*?"

"Well . . ." said Sarah, thinking. "*Myth* is there."

"Right. What about *para*?"

"Paralegal?"

"Sure; which means, *like* legal, similar to legal. What's like a myth, then?"

Sarah wasn't sure.

"A fairy tale," I said.

"Oh." That look of startled recognition that I had seen in Sarah's eyes from time to time.

"And *spera* is the root of our word *vespers*, the evening service in church. So the phrase reads something like this: 'The fairy tale begins, good evening to you.'"

Sarah left that day, thinking, at age thirteen, that Greek might not be so difficult to learn after all. This, I think, is how we pass the tradition on, and it does not require an institution to do it.

As a final example of monastic activity as cultural preservation, consider the case of Olga Bloom, a retired concert violinist who mortgaged her home in 1974 so as to be able to buy an old coffee barge and turn it into a floating concert hall. When longshoremen on the Brooklyn waterfront saw a tiny woman scraping and sawing, they began to help her out. The result was a space that is intimate and acoustically perfect. Chamber musicians love performing in it (twice a week, year-round), and audiences love the low ticket prices and the intimate ambience. One sits in a wood-paneled hall, looking out through four picture windows at the Manhattan skyline. Bargemusic, as the project is called, has sparked a cultural renaissance in the area, one that continues to this day.

Much of the motivation for Ms. Bloom's project came from the fact that we live in a country that does not value the arts, or creativity, all that much. It likes the "winners," the big names, but most musicians don't fall into that category. Most cannot afford to get themselves publicized, or rent a place in which to play, for example; most wind up playing at weddings and bar mitzvahs, even if they are very good musicians. Bloom decided she wanted to create a space where these artists could get away from the "cultural mass production" of American society, and she has managed to help talented but unknown people do some really creative work. She herself lives on Social Security and takes no salary for her work. "For me," she told the *New York Times* in 1985, "chamber music is the epitome of civilization."

As a third and final category of monastic activity, we might consider the notion of environmental design, very broadly conceived. By this, I am not referring to the ecology movement or trendy projects for saving the earth, but, rather, to work that improves the health of society by altering the mental and visual landscape that we all move in. Most of our cities are visual and psychological wastelands. When they do not look like Flint, Michigan, they are coming to resemble corporate enclaves such as Dallas or Atlanta. No community, no soul, just boutiques and conference centers. But an interesting discussion of creative, monastic responses to this is provided by Tony Hiss in *The Experience of Place*. Hiss remarks on the sensation of peace and expanded peripheral perception that can occur even in a place such as Grand Central Station. He talks about men such as Frederick Law Olmsted, the landscape genius of the nineteenth century who designed places such as Prospect Park in Brooklyn and Central Park in Manhattan. With his intuitive sense of the "broad-band focus of simultaneous perception," Olmsted created park after park that generated a relaxed, unhurried feeling for those who walked through them. Olmsted believed that a democracy had to have "unconscious, or indirect recreation" available in order to work, locales where communicativeness and gregariousness were likely to occur. Such places, he believed, should be low-key, rather than bombastic; decentralized, rather than constructed around unifying elements; communicative, not ceremonial.

Redesigning space, of course, does require organization and expertise. In the case of indoor space, says Hiss, one has to pay attention to lighting, the chemical composition of the air, the arrangement of rooms and hallways. Thus, he seems to favor the notion of American cities setting up "Departments of Expe-riential Protection," which in my view would do the whole thing in. The chances that redesigned space, indoor or outdoor, would resemble Disney rather than Olmsted are far too high. We see this sort of thing now in the south of France, where once-quaint, sleepy Provençal villages, invaded by corporate interests for their potential tourist value, have been turned into "medieval" boutique clusters and convey the appearance of having been laminated. This shift happened in the space of twenty years, and it represents the psychic rape of the environment.

Vital kitsch, however, and environmental degradation can be reversed. Years ago, William H. Whyte wrote that relatively small changes in the environment can have an unexpected cumulative effect. In a countryside situation, for example, we might have a "scenic clearing to open up a meadow, a row of sycamores planted along a riverbank, a screen of signs removed at the crest of a hill." Individually, he noted, these projects can seem trivial, but taken together "these tremendous trifles can have a major impact on the environment." All of this is not a "grand-sweep approach to regional design," he wrote, but "in the aggregate, it is the host of small pictures and the perception of them that is, for people, the true regional design."

An inspiring example of a one-man effort to redesign the environment is that of William Thomas, a physician in upstate New York. Upon becoming director of the Chase Memorial Nursing Home in 1993, Thomas recognized why people would rather die than go to such an institution: They are barren places, cut off from all signs of life. The changes Thomas instituted were purely environmental, and he reduced infection and the use of medication by 50 percent, and the death rate by 25 percent. In violation of New York State law, he brought in 137 dogs, cats, birds, and rabbits, turning the place into a menagerie. He also filled the rooms with plants, and turned the lawns into vegetable gardens. Finally, Thomas installed an on-site day-care center and arranged for older children to spend their afternoons with the elderly. He created, in short, a flourishing world for his patients, and they flourished as a result. (Local inspectors, incidentally, also need to be credited with being NMIs: Realizing that Thomas was breaking all sorts of rules, they simply looked the other way.) Thomas reported on these events in *Life Worth Living*, published in 1996. The previous year, Governor Pataki signed a new law into existence, permitting the possession of more than one pet per person in a nursing home.

In a sense, William Thomas' work is repair, or rear-guard action. The inevitable fallout from a corporate consumer society includes loneliness, alienation, boredom, and sterility of the environment. A healthy society would not have a need for William Thomas in the first place, and his work—more than two hundred nursing homes have adopted his approach—will not alter the structure of our society. In addition, there is always the danger that the project could get Starbuckized, like everything else in designer America: add plants, kids, animals, then water and stir. As I have emphasized, in the trendy Land of Hype, success kills, and Thomas himself has remarked on this danger. Yet all of this notwithstanding, the Eden Alternative, as his project is known, is an outstanding example of monastic activity. After all, Central Park and Frederick Law Olmsted did not stop the corporate juggernaut, either; but what all of this sort of work does is transmit a memory trace of what a culture *can* be about, and how environmental design can enhance that culture. Where this might lead, a century hence, one never knows.

So this is the microcosm, as it were; specific examples of what might constitute the monastic option. We can include in it traditions of craftsmanship, care, and integrity; preservation of canons of scholarship, critical thinking, and the Enlightenment tradition; combatting the forces of environmental degradation and social inequality; valuing individual achievement and independent thought; and so on. But central to all of these examples is the rejection of a life based on kitsch, consumerism, and profit, or on power, fame, and self-promotion. As already indicated, the monastic option, regardless of what it might lead to in historical terms, now needs to be a way of life. An NMI understands that he or she does not *have* to be enveloped by McWorld, by the "skin" of a disintegrating society that is abandoning its values and replacing our cultural heritage with hype and marketing. Instead, you can choose a way of life that becomes its own "monastery," preserves the treasures of our heritage for yourself, and, hopefully, for future generations. And as I have said, visibility is something to be avoided; the activity will remain authentic by being its own reward. I could have picked well-known individuals as examples of the monastic option—figures such as Noam Chomsky, who has been called the "conscience of the nation," or Harriet Doerr, who wrote her first novel at age seventy-three (*Stones for Ibarra*), which won the National Book Award. Sure, there are such people around, and personally, I love them—I think they are fabulous, the more so because many of them are light years away from hype and self-promotion. But to focus on these sorts of figures would be to run the risk of enhancing the hero culture that is part of the barren corporate landscape we inhabit; it is like saying that things are not so bad for the poor because they might win the lottery, or that we really do have a vibrant culture because we have a tiny handful of great artists and thinkers. It is, above all, to potentially mislead, to give the impression that only the great can qualify as nomads, as NMIs, when just the opposite is true: *You and I* can lead the "monastic" life, and we can start to do it right now. And don't worry about being marginalized; this is *good*. As Don DeLillo says, in a culture such as ours, the writer, for example, is likely to be more significant for being marginal. "In the end," he suggests, "writers will write not to be outlaw heroes of some underculture but mainly to save themselves, to survive as individuals." The same can be said of all monastic activities, and of the people who engage in them.

Thus far, I have given the reader a microanalysis of the monastic option by providing a few concrete examples of realistic optimism, the street-level activity that may or may not lead to cultural transformation ten or twenty decades down the road. I want to conclude this book with a macroanalysis, an examination of what a transformed world might look like, and how the next cycle of renaissance—the *dawn* of a new American culture—might fit into that larger picture.

ALTERNATIVE VISIONS

At any given moment in history there are real alternatives.
. . . How can we *"explain* what happened and *why"* if we
only look at what happened and never consider the alternatives. . . . It is only if we place ourselves before the alternatives of the past . . . only if we live for a moment, as the
men of the time lived, in its still fluid context and among
its still unresolved problems . . . that we can draw useful
lessons from history.

—Hugh Trevor-Roper,
"History and Imagination"

Before I discuss the possible social forms of the twenty-second
century, and the cultural renaissance that may accompany
these, it might be worth recapitulating where we have come
thus far in our discussion. I began this book by arguing that
economic and technological appearances to the contrary,
American civilization is in its twilight phase, rapidly approaching a point of social and cultural bankruptcy. The gap between
rich and poor has never been greater; our long-term ability to
pay for basic social programs is increasingly in question; the
level of ignorance and functional illiteracy in this country is so
low as to render us something of an international joke; and

the takeover of our spiritual life by McWorld—corporate/con-
sumer values—is nearly complete. An economic superstar, the
United States is, in reality, a cultural shambles, an "empire
wilderness."

I have also argued that in terms of historical cycles, the
underlying chronology here is not that new. There is simply no
exception to the rule that all civilizations eventually fall apart,
and we are not going to beat the odds, or outflank the historical record. The comparisons with Rome are quite startling:
The late empire saw extremes of rich and poor, and the disappearance of a middle class; the costs of bureaucracy and
defense pushed it toward bankruptcy; literacy and Greek
learning melted away into a kind of New Age thinking, and so
on. A Dark Age descended on Western Europe, and, inadvertently or not, a new monastic order acted as a holding operation, preserving the records of classical learning until such
time as a cultural renaissance was possible. In the eleventh
and twelfth centuries, this material was rediscovered, then
flowed back into the European mainstream, becoming the
lifeblood of cultural renewal. We also saw how certain science
fiction writers—Walter Miller and Ray Bradbury in particular—recognized this process as an oscillatory phenomenon,
and puzzled over the nature of this recurring historical pattern.

In Chapter 3, I tried to solve this puzzle, in a limited way,
based on the notion of a "shadow" component within cultural
renaissance—specifically, the scientism and materialism of
Enlightenment civilization, which, under the relentless
progress of capitalism, turned that program into the corpo-
rate/commercial culture of the twentieth century. This is how
we entered the phase of McWorld, an era of economic tech-
nobrilliance, in which shadow has replaced substance and
where the system's success is actually its failure. Learning, in
particular, succumbs to the orbit of consumer values, and edu-

cation is debased as part of the general process of commodity fetishism.

Finally, I talked about a possible updated version of the monastic option, in which a new kind of monastic order undertakes a critique of this society and a preservation/transmission of the positive aspects of the Enlightenment, not as a political movement but simply as a way of life. Whether we are talking about Michael Moore skewering the polite violence of capitalist greed, or Earl Shorris teaching Plato and Aristotle to ex-cons, or Olga Bloom arranging chamber-music concerts on a barge in the East River, we have examples of people who are quietly transforming the quality of American life, not as part of some political movement or half-baked "Aquarian conspiracy," but simply because of their own commitment to the activity. This may not, of course, actually transform American life, but it might leave a memory trace, a fragment of cultural preservation to be picked up in more propitious times. Only time will tell, and it is, in the early twenty-first century, much too soon to even guess.

As the reader is aware, I have tried to distinguish my own analysis from the feel-good books that predict relatively quick turnaround, or a healing of America that can be accomplished without pain. One book that I *do* admire, because it is not squeamish about positing a coming dark age as a prerequisite for cultural renewal, is Immanuel Wallerstein's thoughtful study, *Utopistics*, which explicitly rejects utopian thinking: "The last thing we really need," he says, "is still more utopian visions." It is usually the case that the greater the ambition of a social scheme, the greater the resulting damage, and Wallerstein is skeptical of the human capacity to make wise collective decisions. ("Out of the crooked timber of humanity," wrote Immanuel Kant, "no straight thing was ever made.") Hence, Wallerstein's interest in what he calls "utopistics": "the serious

assessment of historical alternatives, the exercise of our judgment as to the substantive rationality of alternative possible
historical systems." Such a "science," as it were, analyzes the
constraints on human social systems and the zones open to
human creativity. It rejects notions of a perfect, "inevitable"
future in favor of a historically possible, hopefully better, but
necessarily uncertain one. And what is clear about our current
situation, says Wallerstein, is that the current process of globalization is the final phase of our present historical system, and
that we are entering a dark age of historical transition.

Following the "wave" analysis of the Soviet economist N. D.
Kondratieff, Wallerstein predicts that the early twenty-first
century will see an upturn, a renewed expansion of the world
economy, with increasing opportunities for investment and
capital accumulation. The gap between rich and poor will grow
even larger, creating an even greater polarization between the
core and the periphery. As the ideology of endless capital accumulation ("progress") grows, so will the delegitimation of that
ideology. Nations of intermediate strength in the noncore
areas—Iraq, for example—will be able to challenge powerful
ones in the core areas successfully; and within the West itself,
the lack of decent jobs for nonwhites will pose an increasing
threat as the size of the nonwhite population grows. The rich
will become more and more worried about personal safety, as
in Third World countries right now, and the modern world system will enter a period of continuing crisis and instability.
There will finally be a very large periphery within the core. The
privileged class will try to co-opt these challenges by incorporating the rhetoric of the discontented—ecology, multiculturalism, women's rights—which will give the illusion that serious
changes are under way, when, in fact, the essential relations
of wealth and power remain the same. But ultimately, a dark
era, a system break, is unavoidable, because the system cannot

survive as presently constituted; the strains will have become too great, and finally even co-optation won't work. The outcome of all of this is inherently unpredictable. The successor system may be better, but it may not; it could well be much worse.

Personally, I believe it will be better, but my guess is that that will depend, among other things, on the degree of "monastic" activity going on. Drawing on chaos theory, Wallerstein has a few things to say about the coming dark age that mesh pretty closely with the thesis of the monastic option. Transitional periods, he points out, are not normal times; they are ones in which individual action can have a much larger impact on historical developments than would normally obtain. In stable times, even great fluctuations have relatively small effects (that's what we mean by a *system*). But when systems are far from equilibrium, which is the direction in which we are moving today, small fluctuations can have great effects. The role of monastic activity, in short, becomes unpredictable; it could inadvertently push the system, as it disintegrates, in a new direction. This is not, in my view, a simple matter of free will or voluntarism, because the groundwork has to be laid in a cumulative and evolutionary way for the push to have any real muscle behind it. Nevertheless, it could look surprising when it occurs.

The whole issue of "utopistics," of careful assessments of future possibilities and of monastic activity as the agent for these changes, is the subject of a film made by the Swiss director Alain Tanner in 1976: *Jonah Who Will Be 25 in the Year 2000*. The story takes place in and around Geneva, where, in the aftermath of *les années soixantes*, various post-sixties radicals inadvertently converge in a desultory, unintentional effort to create a better society. The physical centerpiece of the story is the statue of Rousseau, in downtown Geneva, which symbolizes the search for alternatives to the oppression of life in commercial civilization. Marcel pursues organic farming and is dedicated to environmental concerns. Max, a disillusioned Marxist, nevertheless manages to get wind of a development scheme being hatched by the major banks, and he advises small landowners not to sell their property. His girlfriend, Madeleine, attempts to defy the reality principle through her practice of tantric sex; and Marie, a supermarket cashier, quietly charges old-age pensioners lower prices for their food. Matthieu undertakes a project in home schooling, along the lines of a Montessori model, while Marco, a high school history teacher, is committed to presenting monastic alternatives. History is *not* fixed, he tells his students; alternatives are always possible. He has Marie come to class and describe the life of a cashier. He has Matthieu talk about how the economy is manipulated by the rich for their own benefit. He argues that, figuratively speaking, history has "wormholes" through which alternative futures can be discerned, and that the same wormholes that are used by prophets such as Rousseau to glimpse the future are used by historians centuries later, in a reverse direction, to understand the past.

How does it end? For his candor, Marco is fired, and he winds up singing "Cherry Blossom Time" to seniors in an old-age home. Marie gets caught cheating the supermarket and is sent to jail for six months. The alternate school is closed down because Matthieu's employer, Marcel's wife, says she hired him to shovel manure, not teach kids about whales. Despite his modest success in derailing the Swiss banking scheme, Max remains jaded and cynical.

I have shown this film to various classes I have taught over the years, and I am always amazed at how diverse the reactions are, ranging from elation to despair. Is the glass half-full or half-empty? Some students point out that all the experiments failed; others see the various efforts as first steps toward a different way of life. In the film, the crucial point is made by Madeleine, a point we have already stressed: History moves much more slowly than a single human life. If you take the monastic path, as I have said, there are no guarantees. You may open wormholes that a historian, two hundred years hence, may look back through and say, "Of course." As Nietzsche once remarked, "It is the mark of a higher culture to value the little unpretentious truths," for it is these that can add up, and ultimately make a difference. The monastic option is not about a pompous "voluntary simplicity" movement, for example, or an institutionalized Clemente Course, or PBS programs on "spirituality." It is something much more private and much less intentional, and it's about things that last.

The topic of alternative futures is, of course, central to our discussion. Even though necessarily speculative in the extreme, this is the heart of my macroanalysis. For Marco's point about wormholes, or what I think of as loopholes, seems to me to be unavoidably true. This does *not* mean that there are no constraints, that the future is infinitely plastic or somehow purely contingent. That would be voluntaristic New Age pabulum, and we can dispense with that from the start. But the notion of loopholes in history is a reminder that historical inevitability exists only with the benefit of hindsight, and that in reality, things are not carved in stone. *Some* degree of contingency is much more plausible than total historical inevitability, the notion that things had to turn out exactly as they did. A few historians have picked up on this "What if?" approach, as the British historian Niall Ferguson details in his edited collection of essays, *Virtual History*; and it is interesting that within the genre of science fiction, a subgenre, called "alternate history," has arisen to explore that very issue. There are a series of novels that take, as their point of departure, an outcome opposite to that of the historical record. What if the Confederacy had won the Civil War? What if the Axis powers had defeated the Allies? What if the Protestant Reformation had fizzled out, and the Western world was almost completely Catholic? The value of counterfactual historical speculation lies precisely in suggesting that while we can say "Of course" regarding our own historical circumstances, we would have wound up saying "Of course" to a radically different scenario if events had turned out differently. Thus in Kingsley Amis' novel *The Alteration*, we get to contemplate a Catholic world in which freedom of individual expression is sharply circumscribed, but in which the brakes that were put on scientific and technological development have resulted in a less hectic, more leisurely world. In Philip Dick's *The Man in the High Tower*, Germany won World War II—"Of course"—and what appears as aberrant fantasy within this scenario is an underground novel in the alternate history genre (written by the man in the high tower) in which Germany lost—"Of course." The point is that detailed hindsight is not fail-safe in terms of predicting future events. Ruptures certainly have a long, and usually hidden, development, but when they do arise, they can seem to come out of nowhere. In this sense, monastic pathways could inexplicably give rise to a very different sort of world than one dominated by the rules and ethos of transnational corporations. For those living in the former world, it will be as much a matter of "Of course" as it will be for those living in the latter. Just maybe, we need to expect the unexpected.

So let's let our minds wander a bit, and do some unexpected kinds of thinking. The first thing I wish to suggest is that historical eras are not meaningfully bound by literal chronology. The nineteenth century, for example, really began with the French Revolution in 1789, which represented the final break with feudalism and the *ancien régime*. In terms of a coherent mental and political landscape—and one that was relatively free from war, in the Western world—it lasted until 1914, a total of 125 years. World War I, and the Russian Revolution, ushered in a very different kind of world: the final phase of modernism, the age of genocide, the era of angst, anomie, Picasso, and Einstein, and the ineluctable emergence of the United States as the world's only superpower. This constellation, in turn, ended in 1989, when the twenty-first century effectively began. Why do I say that?

It was in 1989 that the clear outlines of a very different sort of world from the one that began in 1914 finally emerged. That year saw the beginning of the end of the Soviet Union, and of the (convenient) organization of the world into two opposing camps. This is the centerpiece of what we call *globalization*. No more a clearly defined world of binary opposition, but a decentralized, fragmented world, in which bitter regional rivalries reemerged and the "enemy" could no longer be unambiguously identified. America thus lost its moral, anti-Communistic, mission, and the vacuum got filled with distractions: a brief, phony "war on drugs," the Gulf War, and a decade of trivial political scandals masquerading as news. Such developments, however, were only temporary. The really new moral mission was global corporate hegemony, the old doctrine of manifest destiny now imported into the economic realm and mapped onto the entire world. As I said in Chapter 1, if the twentieth century was the American century, the twenty-first will be the Americanized century, and it will have its roots in a new global economy, in which consumerism will be a full-blown religion.

The second marker of this new divide was that by 1989, or shortly thereafter, microprocessing technology had begun to redefine the mental landscape of the United States and much of Western Europe. E-mail, hypertext, and the World Wide

Web assisted the globalization process, and the spread of transnational conglomerates, in a number of ways. As the final phase of the Scientific and Industrial Revolutions, the Information Revolution had begun to render reality so abstract that it became completely virtual. Like the texts on a computer screen, in which all information has an ephemeral quality and is seemingly equivalent to all other information, places, people, and organizations were now everywhere and nowhere, simultaneously. The nation-state began to become increasingly irrelevant ("cyberia" has no boundaries), and meaning increasingly horizontal. History, identity, and authorship were now seen as abstract data bits in a new world of an eternal electronic present.

The third factor in the transition to the twenty-first century, the shift from a modern to a postmodern world, is neatly intertwined with the other two. By 1989, what had been an arcane French academic discussion about the world as text and the absence of meaning reached popular consciousness. In dozens of ways, the nihilism of deconstruction played itself out in a new kind of everyday sensibility: The president had become, as I have already said, a kind of corporate CEO, with no moral or personal responsibilities; the individual not only had no identity, he didn't *need* an identity, and could reinvent himself continuously; choices were only a matter of what worked, and therefore had no existential or ethical meaning (and, hence, were essentially equivalent); and finally—leaving religious fundamentalism aside, for the moment—no values were superior to any other values, because there was no such thing as the truth, and therefore all realities were interchangeable, so the major activity became mindless consumption.

As the new era enters its twelfth year in 2000, its three defining characteristics—globalization, cybernetics, and deconstruction—have emerged quite clearly. ("O brave new world / That has such people in't!" wrote Shakespeare nearly four hundred years ago.) Despite the sentiments of those who might (reasonably) wish otherwise, these factors will be with us for most of the new century, and they represent the ideologies of a nation that has lost its moorings. In terms of lived experience, they are making most Americans anxious and disoriented, for they inevitably lead to lives of emptiness and futility. Nevertheless, this configuration cannot last, because it is obviously unstable and transitional in nature. You can talk globalization, virtual reality, and postmodern hype all you want; at the end of the day, there really *is* a social, political, and economic world out there that remains nonvirtual and that cannot be deconstructed. We saw this when the Southeast Asian economy collapsed in 1998, and overnight, the middle class was out on the street selling fruit and shoelaces. Similarly, when the electricity is off, the supermarkets are closed, and the militia is patrolling the streets to maintain order, hitting the "delete" button, reading Jacques Derrida, or listening to the current crop of cultural gurus is not going to be of much help.

A number of scholars have attempted to see beyond this point into the twenty-second century, when the transitional dark age is over and a new world system is in place. Thus Wallerstein, in *Capitalist Civilization,* projects three possible future scenarios, any one of which could certainly come to pass. The first is neofeudalism, in which the endless accumulation of capital for its own sake has finally been given up, but in which there would be a restoration of rigid social hierarchies in order to ensure political stability. A second scenario is "democratic fascism," in which the world has been divided into a 20 percent elite and an 80 percent everybody else. This was, says Wallerstein, Hitler's vision as well, except that (beyond the virulence of his ideology) he made the mistake of having an elite that was too small in number. Finally, we could conceivably have a decentralized egalitarian world

order, although how we might achieve this—it seems to me
to ignore the realities of power—he never says. In any case, by
A.D. 3000, says Wallerstein, we may remember capitalism, or
the period from 1500 to 2100, as a long transition to a more
egalitarian world, or as an inherently unstable socioeconomic
experiment, after which the world returned to more stable
political forms.

There are, however a number of other possibilities, some
more likely than others. The least likely is the New Age/pop-
ulist scenario I referred to in the Introduction, where some
combination of dedicated, "righteous" activity and shift in spiritual consciousness turns things around in two or three
decades. We might call this the "miraculous" model, based as
it is on wish fulfillment, rather than on any serious understanding of history or social science. Equally unlikely is the
extreme opposite picture, the scenario of a total and rapid collapse, which happened to ancient Mayan civilization, although
the signs were probably there long before the final events. In
the United States, this scenario would involve a descent into
real barbarism, such as is depicted in the film *Blade Runner*.
This is certainly possible, and may even occur to *some* degree
toward the end of the twenty-first century, perhaps for a short
period of time; but the general outlook, it seems to me, is one
of slow rather than sudden disintegration, for this country
seems to be very good at crisis management. That is to say, it
tends to deal with serious problems at the eleventh hour, thereby staving off disaster, although not accomplishing much else.
We might call this the "muddle through" option, in which the
basic goal is just staying afloat. Famine might be avoided by the
manufacture of cheap food from seaweed, for example, and
mass suicide averted by the distribution of a Prozac-like drug.
Muddling through is what we are doing right now, really, but
we cannot expect to do this indefinitely.

Another possibility, and one suggested by the historian War-
ren Wagar (in *A Short History of the Future*) as the logical result
of the collapse of capitalism, is the rise of a one-world government on a Communist model. This seems a bit dated now;
spheres of influence in, say, three major political blocs seems
much more likely. But the idea is that the only force that can
stabilize the world order is just that, a unified, authoritarian
world order. We may drift into it rather than deliberately organize it; indeed, that is what right-wing paramilitary groups in
this country believe is happening, in one way or another. As
much as I detest their anti-Semitism, their white suprem-
acism, and their crypto-fascism, they do have a point: Day by
day, the government accumulates and computerizes more and
more detailed information on all of us—vital stats such as
medical records, income, consumer habits, criminal records,
psychological profiles, and so on—and centralizes it under
one's Social Security number. As we saw above, the logical outcome of this is described apocalyptically by Ira Levin in *This
Perfect Day*, in which a computerized society of chemically
tranquilized citizens is kept docile by a small technological
elite. This model could also be applied to a spheres-of-influ-
ence situation, in which the planet is carved out in geopolitical
blocs (North America, Europe, the Pacific Rim) that together
police the globe Singapore-style and regulate the masses
through organizations such as Interpol.

This would indeed be a horror, and it could be infinitely
stable, given the level of military power collected in the hands
of a ruling class and its technocratic and administrative subor-
dinates. It is, I suppose, very similar to Wallerstein's scenario
of democratic fascism. In Wagar's scheme of things, this eventually becomes so bureaucratic, stifling, and top-heavy that it
breaks up as a result of constant rebellions, issuing out in
Wallerstein's third option, a decentralized egalitarian world

order—what Wagar calls "the House of Earth" (the Green
option, in effect). So we would have Québec, northern and
Southern California, Scotland, Alsace, et cetera, all as separate
political entities. Of course, devolution, or balkanization, can
take many forms, including the neofeudal one described by
Wallerstein. One can imagine a mosaic world of Green, egalitarian, bioregional harmony, or a situation such as that of
medieval Italy, an anarchic collection of warring states. These
little statelets, as it were, could be as repressive as any totalitarian regime.

   We might also contemplate the possibility of what might be
called the "Hellenistic" model, which is based, historically, on
the flourishing of Greek culture across the Mediterranean
basin and eastward during 336–30 B.C. More broadly, this
might be extended to the second century A.D., when Rome
began to take over that vast area and the two cultures began to
blend. Despite recent revisionist writings that have modified
the picture somewhat, the Greco-Roman world of Alexandria
and beyond has traditionally been seen as a melting pot, a
kaleidoscopic civilization that was cosmopolitan and sophisticated. This *looks* like a one-world situation, since everything
was contained under the banner of Greece and Macedon or,
later, the umbrella of SPQR—*senatus populusque Romanus*.
In fact, it was a very rich and complex synthesis of Greek and
ancient Near Eastern intellectual traditions and ways of life.
Because of this creative mélange, the first two centuries A.D.,
in particular, were witness to a remarkable cultural renaissance
in the cities of old Greece and the Near East, when new literary works appeared in every genre, architecture and the visual
arts flourished, and science and philosophy were transformed
by Galen, Ptolemy, and, in the third century, Plotinus. Underneath the facade of Greek, and later Roman, unity lay a complicated mosaic pattern of religious and political sects. Rome,

for example, did not care what these subgroups were doing as long as they did it privately and publicly paid lip service to Roman authority. If they failed to do that—the Jews of Palestine are perhaps the best example—the state moved against them in no uncertain terms. But if they were willing to render unto Caesar what was Caesar's, then these various subcultures were regarded as harmless and allowed to pursue their diverse ways of life. To some extent, that is the situation we have in Europe and North America today, except that the social and economic pressure to conform is so intense as to make any sort of monastic or bohemian activity very difficult to maintain. The dominant culture in the West is totally pervasive; we do not really possess the relative tolerance of the Hellenistic world, and the marginalized in our society are hardly there as some type of artistic experiment. (Even the Harley-Davidson crowd tends to hold down nine-to-five jobs.) But this could make monastic activity all the more radical in its impact, because its rejection of our own version of SPQR—namely, the Fortune 500—could conceivably erode the structure from within and push it in a "Hellenistic" direction. This is perhaps not the ideal outcome of monastic activity, but I cannot help thinking that this model would hardly be the worst possible future for the Western world, at least for a time.

And finally, we come to the oscillatory model, or the model of disintegration-cum-renaissance, which I have consistently been arguing for. (In reality, this is a metamodel as well as a model, since it can include most of the other scenarios described heretofore.) In this scenario, monastic activity would have maximum impact. The idea here, as in the case of Western Europe in the twelfth century, is a slow, coincidental, and unexpected convergence of factors—one of them being monastic preservation and transmission—that generates a synergistic, unanticipated result. This is what alternate history is all about, but here the "What if?" is located in the future rather than in the past. As in the case of Wallerstein's utopistics, there are affinities with chaos theory, in which small fluctuations can have unexpected consequences. I am not sure what the other factors would consist of, and that is no small point. We know them for the twelfth century; we can only guess at what they might be for the twenty-first. But if we just consider the monastic option by itself, for a moment, in this scenario Michael Moore's films (along with David Barsamian's radio programming, and so on) lead to such ridicule of corporate life that millions of young people refuse to enter it, and business activity in general becomes not obsolete—that would be both impossible and undesirable—but something one is not willing to organize one's life around. Olga Bloom's barge concerts lead to hundreds of thousands of paid careers in music. Will Fitzhugh's journal creates a widespread desire for creative intellectual work. The example of the Clemente Course stimulates people to read Jane Austen, not spend their lives surfing the Web. Is this a total fantasy? Quite possibly, but something like this did happen in the twelfth century, as we saw in Chapter 2. I am talking about minute changes that accumulate over time, after all; it is not as long a long shot as one might think. And it is important to remember that even if monastic activity is not a sufficient condition for this to occur, it is nevertheless a *necessary* one. This is the ideal result of such activity, that by this unexpected convergence of factors we get a recovery of the Enlightenment, but, of course, in an updated, post-postmodern form.

Just for the fun of it, let us say this actually happens. What, then, would be the defining characteristics of the New Enlightenment? We might do well to review the characteristics of the old one first. There are many, of course; thousands of books have been written on the subject. But perhaps the key concept, according to the Scottish historian David Daiches, was that of improvement. We know better now, I suppose; obviously, an oscillatory theory of history cannot include the notion of unlimited improvement, and I shall say more about the reflexive quality of our contemporary knowledge below. But as far as the eighteenth century goes, this was an age of optimism, because it held that knowledge of the natural world, the individual, and society would inevitably improve all three of these. If it was not quite knowledge for knowledge's sake; neither was it strictly utilitarian. Rather, the Enlightenment philosophers believed that the open-ended and disinterested inquiry into these three areas would naturally lead to what Francis Bacon called "the relief of man's estate."

When one thinks of a renaissance, or a New Enlightenment, it seems clear that it cannot be a simple repetition of the eighteenth century. Too much has happened between then and now, and many of our needs are very different from what they were then. Many, but not all. I imagine, once again, a vibrant middle class, strong continuity with Enlightenment traditions of democracy and expanding intellectual inquiry, and a culture in which the arts, sciences, and literature play a central role in the lives of a very large percentage of the population. I also imagine a civilization with strong humanistic values, in which business and cybertechnology play an ancillary role. The world of commerce and video display terminals would be, in the New Enlightenment, regarded as a *tool* of the good life, but no one would make the mistake of confusing it *with* the good life. Accordingly, corporations would exist on a much smaller scale than they do now, and their influence would be correspondingly diminished. Indeed, it couldn't be otherwise, because after the Great Collapse of the late twenty-first century, it would become clear to everybody that corporate control of our lives was a toxic arrangement, finally responsible for the crash, and that now, during the period of reconstruction, it must be avoided at all costs. Along with this, then, there would be a healthier balance between global and regional culture. For one thing, McWorld, and the Coca-colonization of the planet, would be things of the past.

I am not, however, assuming that these changes will come about as a result of a "new consciousness" or spirituality, or some form of willful populist activity. Certainly, there will have to be a change in attitude regarding many things, and certainly, people will have to act in deliberate ways. But the motivating factor behind these changes will be the enormity of the Great Collapse, which will act as a wake-up call on an unprecedented scale. In addition, transnational corporations and their control and saturation of the environment will not be possible because they will be so financially devastated; the resources will not be there for them to do too much mischief. In such a context, monastic values will not seem so odd anymore, and will not be so marginal.

If the twenty-second century brings with it a return to Enlightenment values, it will not be in the sense of coming full circle. As I said, too much has happened since the eighteenth century. The return will resemble a helical motion, incorporating some Enlightenment ideals, but having absorbed enough awareness to push it to a higher level, as it were. And much of what it will have absorbed is the positive contribution of the postmodern assault. We cannot possibly stage a simple revival of the Enlightenment, because if we know the power of that worldview, we also know its limits. The Enlightenment vision of unlimited improvement, and total knowledge of the world, is no longer credible. The notion that one day all knowledge will be unified in a few basic principles; that we can, as a result, completely understand what makes individuals and societies function; and that, on that basis, we can create a better life for all is just not tenable any more. Those who lived during the Enlightenment believed we could know everything. Postmodernists made the mistake of believing we could know nothing. The truth, surely, is that we can know *some* things, and that that knowledge is worth having. Hence, a certain détente is possible between the Enlightenment and postmodernism. The contribution postmodernism has made to Western philosophy is an issue that has certainly been raised before (if not with such virulence): There is a reflexive quality to all of our knowing. If we discover the truth, there is also a subjective component by which we create it, and so we need to maintain an awareness of ourselves as pursuers of truth. We have agendas (not necessarily political ones, I hasten to add) in pursuing the truth, and this will always raise the question of how true that "truth" really is. While it does seem to be the case that $E = mc^2$ and that Galileo's description of projectile motion was right, while Aristotle's was wrong, and that this really *is* universal knowledge valid for all time, it remains the case that much of what we know is culturally and temporally conditioned. The trick, as it were, is to pursue the truth with all the optimism and love of reason that animated the Enlightenment, while at the same time being willing to give the effort a postmodern wink: The knower is part of the known, and the knowledge is probably provisional. I seek the truth, *and* I am aware of myself as a culturally situated seeker of the truth. Granted, postmodernism rapidly degenerated into a terrible, narcissistic hubris; but stirred in with Enlightenment values, it might enable those of the New Enlightenment to cultivate humility with regard to fixed positions on the nature of truth.

There is an old joke that asks, "What do you get when you cross a deconstructionist with a mafioso? Answer: someone who makes you an offer you cannot understand." In his book *Consilience*, E. O. Wilson proposes the following as a philosophical rule of thumb, one that I think will work well for the New Enlightenment: "To the extent," he writes, "that philosophical positions both confuse and close doors to further inquiry, they are likely to be wrong." This describes postmodernism very well, and yet, as Wilson admits, the whole venture cannot simply be "relegated to history's curiosity cabinet alongside theosophy and transcendental idealism." For texts are often indefinite, and multiple viewpoints and interpretations often possible. The postmodern rebellion against fixed forms finally leaves a positive legacy: Beware of fixed forms. Yes, it was a sledgehammer to crack a nut, but let us give credit where credit is due.

So reflexive thinking will be part of the consciousness of the New Enlightenment. I certainly think that is congruent with the monastic/nomadic outlook on life. In an article entitled "The Spectrum of Loneliness," Ernest Becker argues for the monastic outlook as as a kind of destiny for humankind, in which the individual reflexively sees through his or her own cultural conditioning and refuses to be blindly driven any longer by the heroic program of power and achievement. At this point, of liberation from the conditioning of culture, the individual comes face-to-face with the problem of the meaning of life, and can find no secure answer. He may be led to ask, as Becker is, "What kind of social forms can we begin to imagine, in which the loneliness of individuation could be considered a desirable developmental goal in one's personal life . . . ?" He must, as a result, live life as a kind of question mark, and, writes Becker, "It is only at this point that one can speak of an authentic religious consciousness for our time. . . ." That is why the monastic option is sacred as well as secular, in my view: It combines the Enlightenment search for truth with a radical unknowing. Becker points out that this dilemma is probably why the German sociologist Max Horkheimer (see

Chapter 3) was led to speak of "communities of the abandoned" as the proper level of consciousness for modern man.

There remains, nonetheless, the question of whether healthy elitism—what we should really start referring to as "quality"—can be democratized without being destroyed. How many can escape cultural conditioning? How large can these "communities of the abandoned" reasonably expect to be? This was ultimately the question lurking in the literature discussed in the Intermezzo, and it brings me to the final issue I need to address—namely, the issue of power. Unless the human race can really break with the post-hunter-gatherer tendency to deal with its fear by means of wielding power, the post–Great Collapse society I have described probably will not amount to anything more than more wishful thinking. We could still have a New Enlightenment, to be sure, but only within the context of a hierarchical social organization, or, at best, the Hellenistic model described above. I have to confess that I am not thrilled by either of these possibilities. Let me, then, conclude this discussion with a few words about power and its relationship to the human condition.

It was Rousseau's belief that the problem of social inequality—which is to say, the problem of power—was characteristic of human beings *in civilization*. We now know that he was wrong, but only partly wrong. Because of prolonged infant dependency, and the human psychological configuration of self/other separation that usually begins in the third year of life, the will to power is part of our biological and psychological makeup, but it tends to get triggered in civilization much more than in hunter-gatherer cultures. In a brilliant bit of ethnography, Pierre Clastres argued (in *Society Against the State*) that such cultures had a complex and paradoxical way of keeping the will to power in check. I discuss this at length in a previous work, *Wandering God*, and as it is a fairly elaborate argument,

I cannot really repeat it at this point. For our present purposes, however, it is sufficient to say that returning to a hunter-gatherer state, complete with its complex "leveling mechanisms" to prevent social inequality, is not a very likely possibility. This raises the question of what *would* work. In his *Short History of the Future*, Wagar projects a scenario in which altruism and an accompanying lack of interest in power are programmed into human beings by means of genetic engineering, creating a new species, *Homo sapiens altior*. His assumption is that no religion or spiritual discipline will ever manage to do this. Rather, along the lines of Anthony Burgess' *A Clockwork Orange*, we would have to invade the personality scientifically in order to produce changes this radical in nature.

Ira Levin, as we saw, tackles the same question, arguing that rebels or revolutionaries typically want to overthrow the power elite only to install themselves as the new one. What makes his heroic (and antiheroic) protagonist Chip different from all the others is that he seeks not to replace the powers that be but to do away with power as such. Within civilization, at least, this is surely a utopian vision, for it is unlikely that more than a handful of people will ever form "communities of the abandoned" and not start playing power games within these communities (hence Gilles Deleuze's apt phrase, "the microfascism of the avant-garde"). A politics of such saintliness would create a power vacuum, and this could get filled by the worst elements of society, rather than by the best. Short of genetic engineering, NMIs are probably going to remain, as E. M. Forster effectively said, the seasoning of society, never the meat and potatoes.

This brings me to one more alternative scenario, one I am not that happy to consider, but which stands out as a real possibility: Marge Piercy's vision of a three-tiered society in her futuristic novel, *He, She and It*. As in the case of Wagar's scenario, change is possible, according to Piercy, only because of an apocalypse: once again, nuclear war. But whereas Wagar envisioned a progression from a one-world socialist formation to a decentralized egalitarian world (finally made possible by genetic engineering), Piercy's vision is that the corporations manage to reconstitute themselves, and that the United States is then divided into a small, well-behaved technological elite and a huge mass of people living in a poor, chaotic, and unsanitary megalopolis known as "the glop." There is, however, one exception to this—namely, a community of monastic rebels, called Tikvah (the Hebrew word for "hope"), which lives by its own rules, neither succumbing to the sterility of corporate life nor to the anarchic misery of the glop. These rebels pursue lives of meaning and self-awareness, and might be considered exemplary bearers of what I call the New Enlightenment. Their trump card—that is, the reason that the corporations do not take them over or destroy them—is that they are software geniuses, producing "rebel" programs that enable them to protect themselves. So in this scenario, we do have a renaissance, a preservation and transmission of Enlightenment culture, but only for a select few, and their impact on the rest of the culture is apparently nonexistent. Piercy's vision is thus one of a single zone of intelligence in an otherwise depressing world. This could well be what the twenty-second century will look like, and it is perhaps as likely a model as any of the others in this chapter; but in terms of the larger society, it would be a very limited sort of renaissance.

Given this survey, I think we have before us a fair range of possibilities. Within civilization, at least, these are probably most of the basic choices that are available to us, although one can obviously never know for sure. Having said that, let us remember that the monastic option is not intrinsically about these larger political outcomes. I have reviewed these possibilities in order to give the reader some sense of what this kind of macroanalysis might suggest. Many of us want to peer over the next horizon, to have a sense of how it will all come out, so to speak. But ultimately, we need not worry too much about the larger picture, because we have very little control over the future anyway; and even if we did, given the oscillatory schema that civilization is probably forever condemned to live with, the long-term configuration is just going to be whatever it is, with fluctuations of light and dark over long periods of time. This is certainly not the Enlightenment view of the history of humankind, but that may be one of the things we know now, that we didn't know back then. The British philosopher Stuart Hampshire says it better than I can:

> If the supernatural claims about the Creator's intentions are dismissed, there remains no sufficient empirical reason to believe that there is such a thing as the historical development of mankind as a whole. . . . What we see in history is the ebb and flow of different populations at different stages of social development, interacting with each other and exhibiting no common pattern of development. Using older historical categories, we can reasonably speak of the various populations flourishing and becoming powerful at some stage and then falling into decadence and becoming comparatively weak; and historians can reasonably look for some general causes of these rises and falls. Even if some such general causes can be found, they will not by themselves point to a destiny, and to an order of development, for mankind as a whole.

And that is the "end" of our story, and of the possibilities, both micro and macro, of the monastic option in the twenty-first century. I leave it up to you to decide if the glass is half-full or half-empty, or whether that even matters. For the "monk" of the twenty-first century will not be pursuing his or her activity for grand, heroic outcomes, but for the sense of worth and meaning that the activity itself contains. The work may lead somewhere; it may not. Our job is only to give it our best shot. Lew Welch, a San Francisco Beat poet of years gone by, put it this way:

What strange pleasure do they get who'd

wipe whole worlds out,

ANYTHING,
to end our lives, our

wild idleness?

But we have charms against their rage—
must go on saying, "Look,
if nobody tried to live this way,
all the work of the world would be in vain."

And now and then a son, a daughter, hears it.

Now and then a son, a daughter

gets away

As an old Quaker saying puts it, "Let your *life* speak." In the end, that's the only thing that really matters.

NOTES

Note to the reader: In the interest of simplifying the scholarly apparatus used in this book, I have, in the citations that follow, omitted those sources already mentioned in the text, and have not (for the most part) provided references for quotations that are relatively brief. The sources occur in the order in which they are drawn upon.

INTRODUCTION

Thomas Frank, "Dark Age," in Thomas Frank and Matt Weiland (eds.), *Commodify Your Dissent* (New York: W. W. Norton, 1997), p. 272.

Niall Ferguson (ed.), *Virtual History* (London: Papermac, 1998), p. 1 (quotation from Lewis Namier).

Katharine Washburn and John Thornton (eds.), *Dumbing Down* (New York: W. W. Norton, 1996), p. 35 (quotation from Garrison Keillor).

Earl Shorris, *New American Blues* (New York: W. W. Norton, 1997), p. 352 (quotation from Robert Maynard Hutchins).

CHAPTER 1

(a) Section on social inequality

John Cassidy, "Who Killed the Middle Class?" *The New Yorker*, 16 October 1995, pp. 113–24, and "Wall Street Follies," *The New Yorker*, 13 September 1999, p. 32.

Robert Reich, "My Dinner with Bill," *The American Prospect*, no. 38 (May/June 1998), pp. 6–9.

Paul Krugman, "The Spiral of Inequality," *Mother Jones*, November/December 1996, pp. 44–49; see also Kathy Sawyer, "Poorest Families Are Losing Ground," *Washington Post*, 22 August 1999, p. A7, and George Hager, "Study Reports Record U.S. Income Gap," *Washington Post*, 5 September 1999, p. A8.

William Finnegan, *Cold New World* (New York: Random House, 1998), pp. xiii, xvii, 343–50, and 353–56. See also Earl Shorris, *New American Blues*, pp. 391–93, and Gerry Spence, *Give Me Liberty!* (New York: St. Martin's Press, 1998), pp. 60–61, 77, and 185.

Joel Millman, "Mexico's Billionaire Pyramid," *Washington Post National Weekly Edition*, 5–11 December 1994, p. 25.

David Rieff, "Therapy or Democracy?" *World Policy Journal*, vol. 15, no. 2 (Summer 1998), p. 68.

"Number of Poor Children Rises 22%," *Seattle Post-Intelligencer*, 23 March 1992, p. A3.

"India's Child Slaves," *International Herald Tribune*," 17 October 1996, p. 10; cf. similar articles in *Seattle Times*, 22 January 1997, p. A7.

Carol Henson, "Child Labor Figures Nearly Double Earlier World Estimate," *Seattle Post-Intelligencer*, 12 November 1996, pp. A1 and A6.

Christopher Chase-Dunn, "The Effects of International Economic Dependence on Development and Inequality: A Cross-National Study," *American Sociological Review* 40 (1975), 720–38.

Melanie Conklin, "Terror Stalks a Colombian Town," *The Progressive*, February 1997, pp. 23–25; for a discussion of similar CIA activities in Guatemala, see John M. Broder, "Clinton Offers His Apologies to Guatemala," *New York Times*, 11 March 1999, p. A1.

Associated Press releases on the Internet, 21 January 1997, 5:22 P.M. and 10:01 P.M. EST (on Alan Greenspan's congressional testimony).

"Congress Approves GOP Plan to Cut Taxes," *Washington Post*, 6 August 1999, pp. A1 and A6.

(b) Section on entitlements

National Center for Policy Analysis: five reports on-line (www.ncpa.org): "Future Burden of Elderly Entitlements"; testimony by John C. Goodman to Subcommittee on Social Security of the House Ways and Means Committee; 1996 Cato Institute study by Mark Weinberger; "A Summary of the 1999 Annual Social Security and Medicare Trust Fund Reports" (also available at www.ssa.gov); and "Social Security Problems Accelerating," by Bruce Bartlett.

Amy Goldstein, "Prognosis Better for Medicare, Social Security," *Washington Post*, 31 March 1999, pp. A1 and A4.

David Koitz and Geoffrey Kollman, "The Financial Outlook for Social Security and Medicare," *CRS Report for Congress* no. 95–543EPW, 1 April 1999.

David Koitz, "Social Security Reform," *CRS Issue Brief* no. IB98048, 31 March 1999.

(c) Section on loss of intelligence

Gary Younge, "Bill's Home Run in the Big Easy," *The Observer* (London), 27 October 1996, p. 19.

Peter Sacks, *Generation X Goes to College* (Chicago: Open Court, 1996), p. 109 (citing *Time* magazine poll).

Anne Cronin, "America's Grade on Twentieth-Century European Wars: F," *New York Times*, 3 December 1995, sec. 4, p. 5.

Jeffrey D. Wallin, "Is College Tough Enough," *AALE Newsletter*, vol. 2, no. 2 (Winter 1996–1997), p. 5.

Lewis H. Lapham, *Waiting for the Barbarians* (London: Verso, 1997), pp. 63 and 162.

"Teens Ignorant About Government," *Washington Post*, 3 September 1998, p. A19.

Andrew Ferguson, "Failing to Fail Students Part of a Dumbed-Down

Culture," *San Antonio Express-News*, 24 October 1993, p. 4F.

Jane Healy, *Endangered Minds* (New York: Simon & Schuster, 1990), pp. 16 and 20.

"Study of Science Skills Gives Americans Bad Grade," *Kansas City Star*, 24 May 1996, p. A4.

Diane F. Halpern, "The War of the Worlds," *Chronicle of Higher Education*, 14 March 1997, pp. B4–5.

Alvin Kernan, *In Plato's Cave* (New Haven: Yale University Press, 1999), p. 239; James Twitchell, *Carnival Culture* (New York: Columbia University Press, 1992), p. 268.

Paul Fussell, *BAD, or The Dumbing of America* (New York: Summit Books, 1991), pp. 190–94.

Serge Halimi, "US Press Obsessed with Local Issues," *Le Monde diplomatique*, English (on-line) edition, August/September 1998.

"Welcome to Teacher Testing," *Washington Post*, 10 July 1998, p. A24.

Pamela Ferdinand, "Nearly Half of Aspiring Teachers Fail Latest Massachusetts Test," *Washington Post*, 13 August 1998, p. A6.

Kernan, *In Plato's Cave*, pp. 239–40 (on SAT scores).

Mark Edmundson, "On the Uses of a Liberal Education: I. As Lite Entertainment for Bored College Students," *Harper's*, September 1997, pp. 39–49.

Cullen Murphy, "Starting Over," *Atlantic Monthly*, June 1991, pp. 18–22.

Kent Carroll, "The Facts of Fiction and the Fiction of Facts," in Washburn and Thornton, *Dumbing Down*, pp. 224–33.

Doreen Carvajal, "HarperCollins Cancels Books In Unusual Step for Industry," *New York Times*, 27 June 1997, pp. A1 and C3.

———, "Middling (and Unloved) in Publishing Land," *New York Times*, 18 August 1997, pp. C1 and C6.

Benjamin Barber, *Jihad vs. McWorld* (New York: Ballantine Books, 1996), pp. 124–26.

Charles Derber, *Corporation Nation* (New York: St. Martin's Press, 1998), p. 4.

Mark Crispin Miller, "And Then There Were Seven," *New York Times*, 26 March 1998, p. A27.

Kernan, *In Plato's Cave*, pp. 2, 250, 272, 290–291, and 294.

Alain Finkielkraut, *The Defeat of the Mind*, trans. Judith Friedlander (New York: Columbia University Press, 1995; orig. French ed. 1987), p. 118.

(d) Section on loss of spirit

James Twitchell, " 'But First, a Word from Our Sponsor': Advertising and the Carnivalization of Culture," in Washburn and Thornton, *Dumbing Down*, p. 198.

Bruce Barcott, "The Trip to Boundless," *Seattle Weekly*, 26 February 1997, pp. 27–31.

Mark Edmundson, "On the Uses of a Liberal Education," p. 46.

"Important Book Industry News from the Book Industry Study Group, Inc., 23 August 1999," press release posted at www.bookwire.com/bisg/pressrelease99.html (the figure of 0.77 percent is based on category estimates of publishers' units; total books sold equals 2,402.3 million, of which 18.5 million were university press books).

Sven Birkerts, *The Gutenberg Elegies* (New York: Fawcett Columbine, 1995), p. 184.

David Denby, "In Darwin's Wake," *The New Yorker*, 21 July 1997, pp. 50–62.

Michael Oreskes, "That Woman," *New York Times Book Review*, 4 April 1999, p.6.

Judy Mann, "From the Hill, Evidence of Our Decline," *Washington Post*, 29 January 1999, p. C11.

Jeffrey Toobin, "Pat 'n' Bill," *The New Yorker*, 8 February 1999, pp. 28–32.

David Denby, "The Moviegoers," *The New Yorker*, 6 April 1998, pp. 94–101.

David Rieff, "Therapy or Democracy?" p. 66.

David Remnick, "In the Capital of Words," *The New Yorker*, 22 and 29 June 1998, p. 136.

David Remnick, "Exile on Main Street," *The New Yorker*, 15 September 1997, p. 48 (quotation from Don DeLillo).

CHAPTER 2

Mortimer Chambers (ed.), *The Fall of Rome* (2d ed.; New York: Holt, Rinehart and Winston, 1970), essays by J. B. Bury (pp. 13–20), M. I. Rostovtzeff (pp. 67–73), Meyer Reinhold (pp. 74–82), and A. H. M. Jones (pp. 101–7).

Joseph A. Tainter, *The Collapse of Complex Societies* (Cambridge: Cambridge University Press, 1990), pp. 128–52.

Charles M. Radding, "Evolution of Medieval Mentalities: A Cognitive-Structural Approach," *American Historical Review*, vol. 83, no. 3 (June 1978), pp. 577–97.

Hugh Trevor-Roper, *The Rise of Christian Europe* (London: Thames and Hudson, 1965), pp. 88–89 and 98.

Roger Collins, *Early Medieval Europe 300–1000* (New York: St. Martin's Press, 1991), pp. 221, 229, and 232.

David Nicholas, *The Evolution of the Medieval World* (London: Longman, 1992), pp. 78–79 and 320–22.

Lowrie J. Daly, *Benedictine Monasticism* (New York: Sheed and Ward, 1965), pp. 5–7, 63–64, and 268–78.

Charles Homer Haskins, *The Renaissance of the Twelfth Century* (Cambridge, Mass.: Harvard University Press, 1971; orig. publ. 1927), p. 33.

M. D. Knowles, "The Preservation of the Classics," in Francis Wormald and C. E. Wright (eds.), *The English Library before 1700* (London: Athlone Press, 1958), pp. 136–47.

Morris Berman, *Coming to Our Senses* (New York: Simon & Schuster, 1989), Ch. 6.

Robert L. Benson and Giles Constable (eds.), *Renaissance and Renewal in the Twelfth Century* (Cambridge, Mass.: Harvard University Press, 1982), Introduction (pp. xvii–xxx) and articles by R. W. Southern (pp. 113–37), John Baldwin (pp. 138–72), J. H. Mundy (pp. 229–47), and Janet Martin (pp. 537–68).

D. D. McGarry, "Medieval Education," *New Catholic Encylopedia*, vol. 5 (1967), pp. 112–16.

Kenneth Minogue, "The Ego and the Other," *Times Literary Supplement*, 8 January 1999, pp. 3–4.

CHAPTER 3

Paul Mantoux, *The Industrial Revolution in the Eighteenth Century*, trans. Marjorie Vernon (rev. ed.; New York: Harper and Row, 1961).

D. S. L. Cardwell, *Steam Power in the Eighteenth Century* (London: Sheed and Ward, 1963).

William Leach, *Land of Desire: Merchants, Power, and the Rise of a New America* (New York: Pantheon Books, 1993), p. 382 (quotation from James Rorty).

Janet Abu-Lughod, "Restructuring the Premodern World-System," Fernand Braudel Center, *Review*, vol. 13, no. 2 (Spring 1990), pp. 273–86.

Robert Kaplan, "Was Democracy Just a Moment?" *Atlantic Monthly*, December 1997, pp. 55–80.

Susan Haack, *Manifesto of a Passionate Moderate: Unfashionable Essays* (Chicago: University of Chicago Press, 1998), pp. ix, 4.

Peter Applebome, "Education.com," *New York Times*, 4 April 1999, sec. 4A, pp. 27–28.

David F. Noble, "Digital Diploma Mills," three articles (1997–98) posted at www.communication.ucsd.edu/dl; quotations from Leavitt and Loflin are in the first and second of these essays, respectively.

Rosemary Hill, "Explorations of a Third Space," *Times Literary Supplement*, 23 April 1999, p. 18.

CHAPTER 4

Todd Gitlin, "The Liberal Arts in an Age of Info-Glut," *Chronicle of Higher Education*, 1 May 1998, pp. B4–5.

R. H. Blyth, *Haiku* (4 vols.; Tokyo: Hokuseido Press, 1949–52), 4: 290 (quotation from Bashō).

E. M. Forster, *What I Believe* (London: Hogarth Press, 1939), p. 18.

Pierre Clastres, *Society Against the State*, trans. Robert Hurley (New York: Zone Books, 1989), p. 26.

Mark K. Anderson, "Alternative Airwaves," *The Advocate* (Amherst, Mass.), 5 November 1997.

"Success," *The New Yorker*, 12 October 1992, pp. 44–45.

" 'Roger & Me' Redux," *Newsweek*, 5 October 1992, p. 79.

Scott Dikkers, "Michael Moore," *The Progressive*, June 1996, pp. 40–42.

John Marchese, "Me: The Continuing Adventures of Michael Moore," *Esquire*, January 1993, pp. 44–47.

"Michael Moore," *1997 Current Biography Yearbook*, pp. 387–91.

Joshua Hammer, "Phil and Roger and Me," *Newsweek*, 30 March 1998, p. 40.

Ana Gutierrez Johnson and William Foote White, "The Mondragón System of Worker Production Cooperatives," *Industrial and Labor Relations Review* (Cornell University) vol. 31, no. 1 (October 1977), pp. 18–30; see also Morris Berman, *Wandering God* (Albany: SUNY Press, 2000), Ch. 7.

Ethan Bronner, "For the Homeless, Rebirth Through Socrates," *New York Times*, 7 March 1999, pp. 1 and 34.

Richard Whitmire, "What It Might Take to Defeat Poverty," *Seattle Times*, 15 December 1996, p. A3.

The Concord Review, P.O. Box 661, Concord MA 01742; and at www.tcr.org.

Denise Foley, "A Labor of Love," *Teacher Magazine*, vol. 1, no. 3 (December 1989), pp. 26–28.

Charles A. Radin, "Concord Review: Great but No Grants," *Boston Globe*, 20 December 1992, p. A46.

Marie C. Franklin, "Scholarly Journal Publishes Students," *Boston Globe*, 9 March 1997, p. D27.

Jay Matthews, "A Home Run for Home Schooling," *Washington Post*, 24 March 1999, p. A11.

Ira Rosenblum, "Bargemusic: Reflection of a Dream," *New York Times*, 18 August 1985, pp. 17 and 22.

Adam Gopnik, "Olmsted's Trip," *The New Yorker*, 31 March 1997, pp. 96–104.

Tony Hiss, *The Experience of Place* (New Yorker: Vintage Books, 1991), pp. 167–68 (quotations from William H. Whyte).

William H. Thomas, *Life Worth Living: How Someone You Love Can Still Enjoy Life in a Nursing Home* (Acton, Mass.: VanderWyk & Burnham, 1996).

CHAPTER 5

Stanley M. Burstein, *The Hellenistic Period in World History* (Washington, D.C.: American Historical Association, 1996).

David Daiches, "The Scottish Enlightenment," in David Daiches et al. (eds.), *The Scottish Enlightenment* (Edinburgh: Saltire Society, 1996), pp. 2 and 5.

Ernest Becker, "The Spectrum of Loneliness," *Humanitas* 10 (1974), 237–46.

John Gray, *Isaiah Berlin* (Princeton: Princeton University Press, 1996), pp. 88–89 (quotation from Stuart Hampshire).

Lew Welch, "This Book is for Magda," in Donald Allen (ed.), *Ring of Bone* (rev. ed.; Bolinas, Calif.: Grey Fox Press, 1979), p. 9.

INDEX

Aaron, Henry, 31, 32
Abu-Lughod, Janet, 120
Adbusters, 140–41
Adorno, Theodor, 103, 107, 114, 119
Aidan, 82
"Alt. U.," 123–27, 129
Alteration, The (Amis), 166
alternative futures, 159, 165–66, 169–76. *See also* Wallerstein, Immanuel, future scenario theories
"Hellenistic" model, 172–73
"New Enlightenment," 174–79, 181
novels about, 165–66
oscillatory model, 120, 160, 173–74, 175
Alternative Radio, 139–40
American culture, 1–2, 13, 47, 88, 159–60. *See also* alternative futures; American educational system; American intelligence; kitsch; "monastic option"; post-

modernism; publishing industry practices; spiritual death
and collapse of civilizations, 14–15, 17–20, 62–63, 121, 160
crisis of, 3, 6, 8, 19–20, 59, 159–60
institutional solutions, 10–12
and energy/vitality, 3–4, 62
and invisibility, 6
and literacy rates, 42
and the media, 2
American economy, 2–3, 27–28. *See also* capitalism; economic disparity; spiritual death, and consumerism
conclusions concerning, 32
and entitlement programs, 29–33
and Latin America, 25–26
and microchip technology, 49, 50
structural problems, 6–7, 69

195

Morris Berman is well known as an innovative cultural historian and social critic. He has taught at a number of universities in Europe and North America, and has held visiting endowed chairs at Incarnate Word College (San Antonio), the University of New Mexico, and Weber State University. Between 1982 and 1988 he was the Lansdowne Professor in the History of Science at the University of Victoria, British Columbia. Berman won the Governor's Writers Award for Washington State in 1990, and he was the first recipient of the annual Rollo May Center Grant for Humanistic Studies in 1992. His published works include *Social Change and Scientific Organization* (1978) and his trilogy on the evolution of human consciousness: *The Reenchantment of the World* (1981), *Coming to Our Senses* (1989), and *Wandering God* (2000) (more information on these is available at the Web site, www.flash.net/~mberman). He lives in Washington, D.C., where he works as a writer and editor and teaches part-time in the Master of Liberal Arts Program at the Johns Hopkins University.